UNDERTONE

UEA Creative Writing Undergraduate Anthology 2019

CONTENTS

Foreword *Jacob Huntley*...V

Editor's Note...VII

It's Not Going to End This Way *Beth Bacon*...............................3

Your Father's Indiscretion in the Nunnery...................................8
Geronimo Bennington-Poulter

Liminality *Meghalee Bose*...11

It is the stars *Ciara Bright*..17

Wishbone *Sebastian Bronson-Boddie*..22

Credible Fear *Elizabeth Brown*...23

Change Here *Hannah Brown*..29

Broken Bubblegum Machine *Amelia Court*................................34

WYRM *Grace Curtis*..35

Mindflow *Alice Davies*..42

Competition *Dylan Davies*...46

Other *Ella Dorman-Gajic*..48

There's No 'I' in 'Denial' *Milo Filtness*......................................56

Midas, No Longer King *Francesca Finch*..................................62

Egg *Jessica Firman*...64

Wikipedia *Jessica Firman*...65

I

Without Water *Willa Froy* 66

The Battle For Britain *Sam Gardham* 72

Theatre *Kasper Hassett* 76

Study of Michelle *Maya Hayes* 77

Faith *Judith Howe* 82

A Day at the Beach *David Hubbard* 83

Sitting Tight *Joe Hull* 92

The Other Side of the Island *Honor Leveson-Gower* 96

You're Impossible (Can't Imagine Life Without You) 98
Dana Liew Qi-e

Bangkok Incense Holder 102
Charles Lobo-Clarke

Grown Up *Chris Matthews* 103

[noun] *Lucy May* 104

The Tragedy of the Man on the Moon *Magdalena Meza-Mitcher* 106

Court *Magdalena Meza-Mitcher* 108

Pillow Talk *Magdalena Meza-Mitcher* 109

Drive *Millie Norman* 110

Remains *Amber Otton-Miller* 116

The End *Cara Ow* 118

The Staircase *Amy Pattison* 121

Marlboro *Flo Pearce-Higginson* 123

How Much is a Life Worth? *Chiara Picchi* 127

Dark Eyes *Johnny Raspin* 134

The Loveliest Sin *Beth Reeves* 139

Pears *Ellie Reeves* 144

And I Feel to be a Cog in Something Turning *George Rennison* 145

21 Days *Saskia Reynolds* 150

The Funeral of Monsieur Hugo *Colin Sheehan* 157

Artefacts *Minty Taylor* 163

Calling Out *Minty Taylor* 165

Kaleidoscope *Sandra Tse* 166

Modern Melancholy *Jess Watts* 173

Holy Mary, Mother Mary *Nyree Williams* 175

Human *Alex Wiseman* 179

Author Biographies 190

Acknowledgements 198

FOREWORD

'There is not an emotion of the heart, which has not its peculiar tone, or note of the voice, by which it is to be expressed.'

– Lindley Murray, *English Grammar* (1795).

Undertones, subharmonics, suggest listening carefully, catching at things subtly or gently there. Hearing is enriched and the listener is rewarded by more than at first seemed apparent. We might celebrate the volume you are now holding in various ways: it's an anthology showcasing the very best of UEA's undergraduate creative writing students; it's vibrant, bold and original writing; it's a beautifully crafted object in its own right.

We could equally appreciate the tonal range of the writing you have before you.

Tone – be it solemn, ironic, wry or dry – is one of those intangible qualities (resonances, maybe) that elicit an affective recognition from the reader. Or viewer. Or listener. We might equally talk of the scent, shading or flavour of a piece of art. The subtle ghosts that float through a piece of writing, haunting the general effect, giving the story or poem its spirit. Modulating sentiments, making the descriptions more luminous, dusting with melancholy, or adding shimmering tints, these are the ineffable traces the writer catches under their pen, the invisible embroidery lining the words, and which we may hear as 'voice'. How the hell do you teach that? Where to use speech tags to create a beat before the character delivers the end of their sentence, or composing the poem so that the sibilance trickles through the stanzas, sure, we can mark that up on the page. Matters of structure might be the focus of the workshop discussion, and the work will be better for it. The writing that gets to us, moves us, is often achieving something tonal, however, something that sounds right, like the satisfyingly precise pure, clear ring of the tuning fork. Most readers have had that delicious experience of a piece of writing that, as G. K. Chesterton indubitably put it, displays the writer's skill of being able to 'pick exactly the right word up on the point of [the] pen'.

Undertone comprises pieces of writing by creative writers who know just the right word, and work these into compositions with filigreed precision.

We would do well to recall that tone (Gr. *teintein*) has an etymology meaning to stretch. The range of creativity across the following pages is a rich scale of diversity, an array of people, perspectives, lives, styles and voices. Each very different, all resounding vibrantly.

Musically, instruments producing higher frequencies of notes are releasing overtones. Undertones, the lower resonances, are subharmonics. Listen carefully. You will like what you hear, here. The sky's the limit.

Jacob Huntley

Course Director for Undergraduate Creative Writing

EDITOR'S NOTE

Undertone marks the sixth edition of the UEA Undergraduate Creative Writing Anthology and, as always, showcases the talented writers on the undergraduate Creative Writing programme. As ever, this project has centred itself around the imaginations and creativity of students at UEA, not just in the writing featured but also the designing, editing, marketing, and sales of this year's anthology.

This year, we had 52 editors – more than ever before – reading through, selecting, and copy-editing the 108 submissions we received. The result is the 48 pieces featured in *Undertone*, which we hope presents the best of the best of writing produced by undergraduates at UEA. One of the greatest parts of the whole publishing process was hearing our editors respond to the pieces so strongly, insightfully telling us why this story was their favourite, or how that poem touched their hearts.

Another exciting part of this anthology has been working on the design; lead by Francesca Giuliani, the design team worked on the aesthetics and typesetting of *Undertone*, doing everything from selecting a typeface and page layout to dotting every 'i' and crossing every 't'. An especially big thank you needs to be made to Mireia Molina Costa, who created this year's incredible cover design and for being so willing to always do more to ensure it was perfect.

This year's anthology has also seen the introduction of two new areas for students to get involved in, Sales and Marketing. Directed by Ellie Reeves, the sales team has worked hard to organise the launch event for this anthology, ensuring it is the best there has ever been. Meanwhile, Alex Paulley has been leading our marketing campaigns across social media to ensure as many people as possible know what exactly *Undertone* is and how they can support the fantastic writing featured inside. We hope the introduction of these teams has ensured students can get the more than just the editorial experience that comes with making a book, but also skills that can be used in so many different areas in the world.

A final thank you also needs to be made to Nathan Hamilton and Philip Langeskov, who have always been there with advice and guidance when we needed it, and also the School of Literature, Drama, and Creative Writing for their funding of this project. The continued interest and support in undergraduate students' writing is a reminder of how wonderful it is to be a part of UEA's community.

We chose the title for *Undertone* because we wanted something that would reflect the range of writing at UEA, whether that be prose, poetry, or script.

However, this title also reflects the variety of ways students have been able to get involved with the publishing of this anthology, whether that be reading through submissions, designing our cover, running our social media, or organising the launch event. There have never been more ways for students to get involved with making this anthology go from an initial idea to the printed book in your hands. We hope all our hard work and effort has paid off, and that you enjoy reading this book just as much we enjoyed creating it.

Eve Mathews, on behalf of the *Undertone* Team

UNDERTONE

IT'S NOT GOING TO END THIS WAY
Beth Bacon

CHARACTER: Andrew Cunanan – 27.
PLACE: Room 205 at the Normandy Plaza Hotel, Miami Beach, Florida.
TIME/DAY: 10pm, July 14th. The night before the murder of Gianni Versace.

Exit located up-stage centre. Art deco style furnishings: a single bed, centre stage; a mirror, stage left and stage right; cut-outs of the news articles about Andrew Cunanan's murders and a photograph of Gianni Versace stuck to a cork board propped up against the bed, centre stage. A stack of fashion magazines and Louis Begley's novel, 'About Schmidt' are stage right of the bed. A leather brief case sits to the right of the magazines and contains a hair trimmer, a screwdriver, a long, sharp pair of scissors, duct tape, Sellotape, and a gun. Clothes lie across the sofa, including recognisable 'Cunanan items', such as his red baseball cap, circular glasses, and a black leather jacket. To the left of the couch sits a ghetto blaster. BDSM equipment (latex face mask with only two holes for nostrils, a whip, and ropes) drapes over the mirror. Andrew stands centre stage. The room is dark and dingy. The light comes from spotlights shining from the floor beside each mirror, up to Andrew's face, and dim stage lighting from above.

Andrew nervously glides hands through lush, brown locks. He is sweating and humming words to 'Bang Bang' by Nancy Sinatra, under breath. Humming crescendos into triumphant singing.

ANDREW
>"Bang, bang, I shot you down! *(raises his hand to the mirror and pretends to shoot himself through the reflection)* Bang, bang, you hit the ground! Bang, bang, that awful sound. *(turns his gun hand to his throat)* Bang, bang my baby shot me down." *(mimicking the sound of a pistol firing, he pretends to shoot himself in the mouth.)* Bang!

Andrew dramatically leaps back and falls on his back pretending to be dead. Lies there for a few moments. Laughs hysterically. Gets breath and jumps into a cow-boy pose, hands on imaginary revolvers on either side of waist. Leaps towards reflection in mirror, pointing imaginary gun at himself.

ANDREW
> *(Whispers)* Bang.

Mood switches and looks lovingly at his reflection.

ANDREW
> Oh, darling. I am so sorry. I didn't mean to. I just… *(beat)* my finger slipped. I promise it won't happen again, OK? *(Beat)* Yes, of course, I love you too.

Slowly caresses mirror and stares at himself lovingly. Takes top off and persona changes as he pretends to be speaking to Lee Miglin in other mirror.

ANDREW
> Lee. Oh, Lee Lee Lee. You dirty, dirty man. Hypersalivation I believe is what they call it. Revolting. You couldn't even control yourself when you were on death's door. Absolutely no dignity. You just let it seep right out of you. I did everything I could to protect your precious head. *(Picks up duct tape)* I wanted to keep it intact. That consideration really came from the heart, you know. *(Wraps duct tape around his head, starting the top of his head, facing the mirror)* I wrapped you up just as George Clooney does on E.R. The doctors call it 'spiral wrap'. Inch by inch you cover the wound. And, indeed, wounded your poor little head was. I knew you needed some TLC. And you were in good hands. Excellent hands, if I do say so myself. I even made a little air hole for your pre-powdered nostrils. *(Gets to nose and tears tape to make hole for nostrils)* They say don't get high off your own supply, but I broke that golden rule for you. You ungrateful son of a bitch. Not only did you leave me high and dry but you also left me a - actually, high and dry is probably the wrong phrase, let's say high and soaking fucking wet – *(Wraps tape from bottom of neck up to mouth)* and with that, you left me a little present, didn't you, Lee. A perfect little gift of penetrative pain that is currently rushing through my veins. My body was *(beat)* perfect. But something has changed. Hasn't it, Lee. Part of you is infecting me. Part of your disgusting, dilapidated anatomy is poisoning my very being. You begged, eventually. But it was a little late, wasn't it, Lee. *(Wrapped all of head apart from mouth. Impersonates voice of sales assistant.)* I am very sorry, sir, but there is a no returns policy with this product. So, I'm just going to have to let the manufacturer know that I am not happy with my purchase. And so, you're going to go bust. *(Tapes up mouth).* Bust, bust, *(shouting)* bust!

IT'S NOT GOING TO END THIS WAY

Rips tape off head, grabs screwdriver and repeatedly stabs pile of tape on floor in fury. Catches breath, snaps out of this persona, and turns around in a flourish to face the bed. Marches towards it and flops down upon it. Picks up piece of paper to side of him: "WANTED BY THE FBI" poster.

ANDREW
> "Cunanan is being sought for an April 1997 murder, which occurred in Chicago county, Minnesota. Also, he is wanted for questioning in connection with additional murders, which occurred in CHISAGO – Chisago? Oh, Chicago! Ha! What dweebs can't even write a fucking WANTED poster without noticing errors right in front of their fucking eyes! – ChiCAGO county, Minnesota; Chicago Illinois; and Pennsville, New Jersey. – Wow, I have been around haven't I, Mr Jetsetter. – Cunanan may be in possession of a handgun." – Oh, why indeed I certainly am!

Picks up gun from briefcase and caresses it.

ANDREW
> Hello, little one.

Kisses gun, place it onto bed. Picks up poster, so audience can see it.

ANDREW
> "Armed and extremely dangerous" – Oh, darling, don't flatter me so.

Smooches poster making loud kissing sound. Grabs duct tape and scissors from briefcase. Carefully places WANTED poster next to mirror and slowly cuts lots of pieces of Sellotape off the roll and WANTED at top of mirror and ANDREW CUNANAN at bottom of mirror. Lovingly looks at self in mirror for a moment or two.

He swivels, walks towards ghetto blaster and plays 'Blue Suede Shoes', by Elvis Presley.

Strides back towards mirror dancing to music. Sticks WANTED poster to mirror using each piece of tape he has cut off in time with each line he sings.

ANDREW
> "Well, you can knock me down, step in my face, slander my name all over the place, well do anything that you want to do!"

Jumps up and pirouettes to the tune, centre stage, then dances. Steps ghetto blaster to turn off.

ANDREW

(Takes cork board over to mirror, stage left, and speaks to pictures of Versace). You are my blue suede shoes. No one can step on you but me. *(Pulls picture off mirror, walks over to brief case and picks up dagger).* I can step on you, of course. I will clutch your throbbing neck, feel the bristles of your chin stubble as I lean in *(Pushes picture against mirror and moves in close)* and whisper in your ear, "This is the end". I will finally penetrate you with Blake – oh, I had to name my little buddy after all his hard work – and your hot blood will pulsate into my palm. *(Pushes blade into cork board and tares Versace picture)* Oh fuck. Fuck fuck fuck! What have I done?! *(In a frenzy, Andrew drops the knife, takes the pieces of Sellotape from the mirror and tries to stick Versace's picture back together).* NO! I can't tarnish you! No! It's not going to end this way. No. I won't make a mess. Not like last time, not like the others. Lee was a God-awful catastrophe. You deserve better than that, of course. *(Sits down comfortably on floor)* I mean, you are THE Gianni Versace. I know I said that if you were Gianni Versace then I would be Coco Channel. Well, of course I didn't mean that. I know you understand. Besides, Coco Channel's current line is just *(dramatically)* wacky and tacky! You know what I mean. This fall's Versace collection emulated boldness and power. Channel, well, you want to know my real view? I mean, honestly, Gianni, level with me. Do you want to know my honest opinion? I think Coco is the one that should be rotting in hell, not you. Why should we liberate women from the constraints of corsets when we can reveal a dark and dirty side to the typical femme? For instance, Elizabeth Hurley. The little black dress would not be the saucy yet essential item it is today without your 1994 safety-pin frock. Anyway, I am not insinuating you will rot in hell. You have changed the world of fashion. Why would Satan wish to burn your ideas in hell when you can make the seraphs sordid? God! The way you brought bondage to the forefront of high-end fashion in your '92 fall line. Wow. Dazzling! No one could have transformed leather throat chokes and body buckles quite like you. I don't know why I have to justify that to your face. You know you're completely on top of your game. Although, I just don't think the world appreciates you as they should.

Walks towards the bed, sits down, and crosses his legs.

ANDREW

What would Gianni do? That is, indeed, the question. *(Holds up Gianni's photograph reflectively)* What would you do, Gianni? Imagine you had spent months crafting those bondage garments and no one batted an eyelash. What would you do? You would be goddamn devasted, would you not? *(Walks over to bed and lies down dramatically)* But that, I guess, is the fundamental difference between you and me. You are Gianni, I am Andrew. Even in the cadence of our names. I just project *(beat)* bland. That's why I must finish what I started triumphantly but genuinely. I must be Andrew. When I look you in the eye and you, finally, look right back, I will be me. For the last time, I will wholeheartedly be Andrew Phillip Cunanan. And I will say to you, Gianni Versace, "You are in the company of the most wanted man in the United States of America." That's not who I wanted you to meet. I wanted you to love for me who I am or was. *(Beat)* I truly did, Gianni. I wanted us to be buddies. But we are fundamentally parts of different worlds. With your family name and mansion over-looking Miami Beach. *(Appreciation turns to jealousy and anger)* I have known plenty of men like you. You are from an exclusive, illusive class. You are THE Gianni Versace. But that does not mean to say there cannot be another. Who will know you are gone when I pop that little nugget into your skull? It'll be seamless. You'll slip away. And in your place, there will be me, and I will become you. Don't worry, I tried with plenty others. But they just didn't quite fit the bill. You know? I'm sure you understand. I mean, you wouldn't hire some stumpy-legged, squash-faced model to front your New York Fashion Week show, would you? So, why would I settle for second best either? I got my revenge. I got the man that gave me the little lurgy in my blood. And now there's only one thing left to do. I will survive. But only through you, Gianni. I cannot survive as bland Andrew anymore. It's not going to end this way. It's not going to end the way it began. I must begin a new cycle, with a new face, and a new name. I have done it before, haven't I? I have succeeded time and again, have I not? I am quite the actor, if I do say so myself. And now I will finally be who I have always dreamed of becoming. I will be Gianni Versace. So, slip away with dignity, please, Gianni. Don't go like Lee did. It will end the way I wish it to end.

Puts on red baseball cap, sets down photograph, and faces audience. Smiles at audience. Turns and slowly picks up belongings and places them into a backpack. Turns back to audience with room cleared up, bows his head to audience, and exits.

YOUR FATHER'S INDISCRETION IN THE NUNNERY
Geronimo Bennington-Poulter

You spent much of your childhood sitting on a windowsill and from there you saw many things that you found quite wonderful. You saw raindrops stop in mid-air, striking an invisible, unexpected surface, sliding down, coming to rest just next to, yet completely out of reach of, your naked feet. You saw sunlight slice through the glass to paint your body gold and as the day grew older, you watched it fill the room with its damp glow. You watched people hurry down the stone path and leave just as quickly: postmen, gas men, plumbers and one or two of your household's few friends. It was only by looking through that window that you knew freedom existed. It was only through seeing those things outside that encouraged you to question why you had to remain inside, encouraged you to ask your mother why you were never allowed to leave the house.

And when you did: "You know why." She answered you unsatisfactorily from her rocking chair, her knitting needles clicking wearily along under her frayed silky voice. "No, I don't." Your ten-year-old self replied. "Because of your Father's indiscretion in the nunnery."

And she glanced over at your Father, a handsome and well-aged man. He was looking intently at his paper, pretending he hadn't heard.

But he had heard.

And you knew he had heard because on his well-formed features was fixed an expression of deep shame and embarrassment.

And yet, looking past that, it looked to you as though he was a little pleased with himself. In fact, not only pleased with himself, but rather impressed with himself as well.

Remember it now, remember it.

Now you think of it, yes, you swear you saw the flicker of a smile scamper across his face.

YOUR FATHER'S INDISCRETION IN THE NUNNERY

So for this reason, and no other reason was ever given to you, you were confined within that house for nearly all of your formative years.

And, because there was little else to do, you spent those years getting to know every corner and every crevice and every nook of the building. You grew to know every carefully decorated room, every furnishing, every ornament, every pattern in every fold of every sheet of wallpaper that clung to every wall. You knew the underside of every bed, the noise of every spring, the whistle of wind through every gap in every window.

And everything you grew to know you grew to hate. You grew to hate the different creaks that each door made when it opened and when it closed. You grew to despise each dull inch and loathe every centimetre of that horrid place.

Remember.

The years crawled on, and everything you knew became foul to you. The click of your mother's knitting needles, once a thing of comfort, seemed cruel and snide, a sinister chattering. The tapestry of cracks on the ceiling that used to charm you to sleep began to seem uglier and uglier as each night passed, and insomnia began to haunt you with increasing nastiness as you moved, stagnant, through the weeks and months and years.

Remember.

When you saw your father smile, it was a smile you had seen a million times before and you hated him for it. When your mother cried it was a cry you'd heard a hundred times and you knew exactly how the creases in her face would guide the tears down her face and it revolted you.

Remember.

Every shape they could contort their faces into was so awful and familiar that eventually you shut yourself in your room, and you cried over the endings of books you'd cried over three or four times before.

And all this because of Father's indiscretion in the nunnery, all those years ago.

It was only when you reached the age of eighteen that you were given your freedom. You were encouraged to stay by your parents, although I'm sure they knew you would not be convinced.

You found yourself a cheap flat in a busy city, you found a simple job and you began to live your life.

Remember.

You approached life in the outside world with the zeal of the convert. You saw possibilities for mayhem and newness that we, with all our years out of doors, could never spot. You promised yourself you would never settle down anywhere permanent. When you could, you went weeks without spending two nights in the same place. You vowed you would travel, and that you would throw yourself at every exciting new opportunity with violence and hunger.

With the end of every short, bright chapter of this new life you charged through, you made new promises to yourself that would force you to push life's boundaries further. Promises that you broke with the same recklessness and glee that you made them.

But throughout all this there was one steadfast commandment that you refused to break no matter what. Wasn't there?

Remember.

You swore that you would never give yourself the permission, no matter what strange and impossible circumstances might occur, to commit an indiscretion, of any nature, in a nunnery.

Which I imagine makes it very hard to explain why you're doing what you're doing right now.

Doesn't it?

Makes it hard to explain why you find yourself here: your naked chest pressed against a stone-cold altar, looking up at great windows painted in wonderful red and green, being savagely, repeatedly, but by no means unconsensually, anally penetrated by sisters of the cloth.

LIMINALITY
Meghalee Bose

The door was rattling under my knuckles. Heedless of the noise, I kept knocking – battering on the flimsy wood till the hinges screeched, and Milt was glowering down at me.

"What?!" I wiped his spittle from my forehead. "Is Mum in?"

"Just stepped out. Took Des with her to the fields – something about gathering stuff for the evening." *Not a speck of mud in the house.* I scrubbed my feet on the mat outside, rubber sandals slapping against my heels. *Not today.* Slipping through the low-hanging doorway, I barely moved ten steps before turning to put my back to the wall.

Milt was still standing by the door, arms folded. I looked above his shoulder instead, the brick peeking beneath crumbling yellow plaster where the door had rammed it one time too many. "We were getting worried." About what, he didn't say. Mum had probably made a racket; how late it was getting and how they couldn't start without me and didn't I know that the ceremony had to take place *exactly* as the sun dipped below the horizon? Flooding the sky with scarlet, contaminating the clouds. Of course, she wouldn't have phrased it quite like that. Not one for poetry, my mother.

Hands stiff by my sides, I resisted the urge to fidget. "I went for a run, that's all." It sounded believable. A one-roomed house, no matter how sparsely furnished, didn't leave much breathing space. Milt's eyes still bugged out, brown and button-like. "Like *this*?" My face steamed up. "I'm not a damned invalid." Steam. Like Mum's old kettle, rattling and hissing vapour and –

"I need your *yalta*." My brother blinked at me, wide-eyed still, gaze dipping to the short-hemmed cloth tied around my waist. "You're wearing one."

Old, leaking, faulty. My tongue rolled uselessly, pressing against hard teeth till it ached, till I'd browbeaten each syllable into existence. "It…stained." *Who told you to go on a run then?* But Milt said none of that, dropping his hands immediately to tug at his longer *yalta*, neatly knotted over his trousers. I could feel the pressure in my jaw ease a little.

"I meant your old one."

All that got me was an incredulous look, and the hiss of cloth as a yard of undyed cotton pulled free. A few seconds of itching silence, and my fingers fell to my own waist, fumbling to undo the knot and all the tiny things I'd been so agonisingly conscious of magnified: the colour in my cheeks, the heaviness in my belly, the stickiness dribbling down my butt crack.

I bunched the stiff cloth between my fists, the dark red smears all too noticeable – dropping it to the floor in a crumpled heap before swiftly knotting Milt's above the navel, as tight as it would go. No time to change my skirt or underthings, so this would have to do. Mum and Des would be home any second.

"Does it hurt?" My joints felt hot and creaky, lower back drawn tight, stomach a pit of roiling acid. I glanced up. My elder brother kept watching me, brows furrowed – the same one who'd cried more when *I* shattered an ankle, soothed my papercuts with saliva-soaked rags.

"No." The lie came easy. "You're being so nice, I'm almost not mad about giving you my books."

Milt did not reply.

*

The actual ceremony of giving away my books wasn't too fussy. We sat around the ritual circle, Mum, Des, Milt and I – though it looked more oblong than anything, hastily drawn on the floorboards with a stub of chalk Des had unearthed. The cross-legged pose was murder on my back, but Mum insisted. She scattered clumps of soil by my knees, freshly dug; if I looked straight ahead, I could almost not see them. *Fertile.* We didn't have a ceremonial dagger, so Milt waved a breadknife around my head instead – two times clockwise, thrice anticlockwise. *Blood.* With every swing, the blunted edge caught a glimmer of the sinking sun outside.

Everything went on without a hitch, until Milt caught sight of my wet cheeks and fumbled. But Mum just scuffed a hand through my hair.

"Only the cramps," she said.

"Today, you are a woman." She intoned, heavy and unreachable.

"You may renounce all that is unworthy of your concern." The books themselves were sitting by my side, half concealed by my thigh – Des had tied them up with a bit of fraying ribbon. I could feel the threads wisping against my skin. "You may move past the threshold, youth to full grown."

LIMINALITY

Three books in all, which was plenty respectable: Nessa, the priest's daughter had seven, all newly bought for her Bleeding. Her parents invited five boys from class, and two more from her prayer group. The school couldn't stop nattering about it – all the boys said they'd gotten the lone hardbound from the set, but confirmation from the source was impossible. Nessa would never set foot in school again.

The priest had explained it differently than Mum. *Today, you are sullied. You may not enter places of worship. You may not enter places of learning.* I hadn't needed to buy books for my Bleeding. Both the ones for school were in pieces, sloppily held together with hoof glue and without page numbers. The third was a creased poetry primer bought with candy-money. I hadn't minded, spending every hoarded grimy penny – not even when Milt grinned smugly in my face, teeth tacky with orange sugar-crystals. I could *read*. Clearly, he'd had the better tactic all along.

"Today, you cast your attention to better things."

Mum slid her hand past my thigh. Broad fingers wrapping around breakable spines, pulling the books out. I didn't protest, because then we'd have to start again from the beginning and Des was sleepy and my chest was dammed up with whimpers I couldn't let out. They landed on Milt's lap with muted thumps, and he blinked at them, hands unmoving. The first night I'd had my primer, I'd slept on it – cheek pressed flat to the cover, breathing the ink in. Milt looked now like he wanted to burn his.

It deserved better. They all did.

*

Come night time, the room was muggier than a drunkard's breath. The air was still heavy with the incense Mum had burned, two whole sticks to purify the Bleeding circle. I watched the leftover embers, orange pinpricks in scattered ash. The floor was cold under my belly, even through the bamboo sleeping mat. Arms folded, chin numb against the ground, I lay prone and watched the lights slowly flicker out. It hurt to move. But it was hard to stop moving: tiny, restless motions that dragged the stiff hem of newly bought cotton against the back of my knees. Seconds tripped by, cold and uneasy, till I finally stilled and gritted my teeth.

"I'll return your *yalta* tomorrow."

From across the room, big brown button-eyes flitted away, ending the staring. Then, low and brusque.

"Don't be ridiculous." My lips pulled, further and further into something sharp I couldn't understand. A caricature of a smile. Silence trailed, as much as the cicadas and Mum's trumpeting snores would allow it. But Milt evidently wasn't done yet.

"Where'd you…where'd you go, earlier? For your run."

"School," I said briskly. The pain didn't feel like it was tearing through my gut anymore. Like how you could only feel the hurt in one part of your body at a time. Mine was still clogging up my chest, tight and impervious. "Sneaked past the gate, climbed up the steps."

"All of them?" All seventy-eight. I knew that because I could recite the alphabet thrice, a letter for each step, three times before jumping off on the zee. I did it every day. And I could swing that thought like an axe, chip away at the hurt and fling it out with my words.

"Rung the bell and everything. The entire school's unclean now."

Milt said nothing to that; I didn't expect him to. My eyes were almost closing, despite it all, when –

"The books are still in the house, you know."

I know. But everything had changed and Milt couldn't understand, not really – and that thought had never struck me so clearly. Like the clang of a bell, a singular note, vibrating in my ears.

Don't talk. Go to sleep. Please.

But my loving brother would not. "You could read them whenever. I wouldn't…you know I wouldn't. Nothing has to…" A pause.

"Or…maybe I could… I don't know the tough words like you do." No one did. I knew the toughest words long before I became the oldest girl still in class. Now that would be somebody else.

"But I could still read 'em out to you?" I turned on my side. What came out was raw, unvarnished truth.

"I would rather die."

*

I came to as they dragged me out of the burning house.

Must have dozed off, though I hadn't expected to. Sleep arrived at the strangest of times. What felt like Mum's clammy hands hooked under my armpits – Des at the other end struggling with my feet – a voice, desperately asking, *"Is this part of the ceremony?"*

No. I wanted to giggle. *Not at all.* But I remained limp and soundless, till the world was stationary again and my legs were dropped unceremoniously to the ground. A couple of beats. I lifted my head an inch, coughed the air out. It smelt of smoke. Laid my head back down, wet grass tickling my cheek. Above and around, people were screaming. At least Mum was – she sounded like a wolf baying for blood. Mourning tones stripped away, terror taking its place – a single-syllabled howl she wouldn't give up.

"Milt! Milt!"

I raised my head again, elbows bending, palms digging into hard ground to bring my body up. It was almost daylight, though it was hard to tell, dawn-pink sky polluted by grey. For all the smoke my house was belching out, I couldn't spot a flame. I watched the smoke, a billowing tower, heart pounding steadily all the while. *Thump-thump-thump,* a triumphant metronome. But then, over to the side – Mum hitched a sob of relief, Des darting into my vision to streak towards the door. There was an outline, amidst the black cloud. An outline growing clearer and darker, coming out.

Milt emerged from the smoke, staggering a few steps before crashing into Des' arms. His trousers were scorched up to his knees, soot-streaked hair tufted to one side. His shoulders shook with the force of his coughs – great big hacking things that seemed to tear through his insides to get out. A couple moments more, and Mum had reached his side too. Even from this distance, I could see her stubby fingers fluttering. Useless, trembling motions, before reaching out to cradle his hands – palm around palm, one pair broad and cupping, one pair burned black.

He shook, she soothed. Half a book tumbled out from his grasp – what hit the ground was more ash than not, charred up to the spine. So caught up was I in wondering which poems had filled those incinerated pages that I almost missed the words, ringing frantically through the air. My poor, distraught mother.

"Why'd you…you shouldn't have gone back in."

But I had to get the books out, Milt didn't say. Or even, it wasn't the incense. The fire started at…the books were burning first.

I hadn't considered he might go back in. It took a particular kind of courage after all, to run into a burning house. Though not as much as it took to start a fire and go straight back to sleep.

Milt turned his head, slow and aching. Searching for me, perhaps.

When his eyes finally found me, I could see that they were red. For a second we stared at each other. Unsmiling and equal.

It didn't feel like guilt. Just a bit like bleeding.

IT IS THE STARS
Ciara Bright

Cass's first solid memory is a tall man, dressed all in black with frogging up the front of his military coat. She's six and he towers over her, green eyes glittering under black caterpillar eyebrows and mouth twisted into a smile that makes Cass feel sick. He bends down from his towering height and attempts to look her in the eyes but she stares at his ear, her eyes darting away from his whenever he tries to reposition her head. Her cheeks hurt where his gloved fingers dig into her face and her skin crawls at the smell of smoke.

After an eternity of fighting, he gives up and leans even closer instead, putting his lips right next to Cass's ear.

"You can't escape your fate, Star Child. One day I won't have superiors to answer to, and I'll have free reign to do with you as I see fit."

He lets go and Cass drops to the floor, wriggling sideways, slithering under her bed. There's a chuckle from above, then she watches the solid black boots walk away from the bed, watches the bedroom door open and close

When her father finds her the next morning, she gets told off for not sleeping in bed like she's supposed to. Cass scrunches her face and taps her fingernails on the table in a rhythm from the theme tune to one of the TV shows she watches after school. Her father sighs and asks her to please sleep on top of the bed tonight. Cass chews the inside of her lip and feels white hot prickles run down her arms, but she cuts the feeling off and nods.

*

Ten years pass in which the only shadows in Cass's bedroom are provided by her imagination and her racing heart. She sleeps on top of the bed every night, but under seven layers of blankets, surrounded by pillows and stuffed toys, trying to hide her form amongst all the other lumps. She has nightmares, waking up with sticky tracks down her face and the same strange heat in her arms and legs, but always stays silent. She knocks her head with her fist until she falls asleep again, counting in sevens all the way up to one hundred and ninety-six.

On her seventeenth birthday she wakes up from a dreamless sleep, lungs already catching, heart already racing, palms already sweaty. She drags her palms along the quilt cover, trying to get rid of the awful, clammy texture, and listens.

She hears everything else, first. Hears the tick of the pink watch on her wrist, hears the wind and the rain outside, the hum of the fridge downstairs, the water in the pipes, the radiator in her room, the hum of electricity from her speakers on her desk. Then she hears the creak out on the landing on the strange patch of floor outside her father's room, and she freezes. It's the wrong type of creak, the wrong weight on it to be her father.

There are socks on Cass's bedside table and she pulls them on, fumbling with fingers that won't keep up with her racing mind. When she slides out of bed, her feet don't stick on the wooden floor, and she arranges the pillows and toys to better suggest the body of a person before darting across to her wardrobe. She curls up in the bottom of the wardrobe, wrapping herself around the backpack she keeps prepped in there, and trains her eye on the tiny gap where the door meets the body of the wardrobe, between the hinges. A bang rings out from the room next to hers and Cass nearly shrieks out loud, the sound echoing around her skull, clattering in her head. She makes more noise herself getting her hands up to her ears, but she's still and silent again before her own door opens.

She has to blink the tears out of her eyes to see properly. A familiar figure steps into the room, dressed in the same black military uniform, bringing the bitter stench of smoke. Cass chews on the inside of her lip and watches, heart in her throat.

The man stalks across the room to the bed, and Cass shifts her eyes to peer through the gap between the two doors, where she can see him standing by the bed. He grabs the blankets and yanks them off, sending pillows and stuffed animals flying everywhere, then pauses at the empty bed.

"Oh? Star Child thinks she's clever."

He shakes his head and kneels to peer under the bed. After a moment, he sits back on his heels. "Hmm. Maybe she has gotten clever." He checks under the desk next, then the built-in cupboard opposite the wardrobe. ù

Cass takes a deep breath. She twists about to get the backpack over her shoulders, trying to make as little noise as possible. The man steps into the cupboard and she explodes out of the wardrobe, diving across the room to slam the cupboard door shut, before spinning away and racing out of her room. She takes three steps down the stairs, then vaults over the banister, landing in a crouch and snatching a pair of trainers from the shoe rack. She doesn't stop to put them on, just runs for the front door and bursts through it.

A van is waiting at the bottom of the road, the triangle logo with stars for points a familiar image that leaves a sour taste in her mouth. She'd done research on the 'Star Child' that the man had mentioned all those years ago and discovered a group obsessed with finding a child born from a fallen meteorite. It's their logo on the van, their uniform on the man. She knows they suspected there was a kid running around with some kind of special powers, knows they want to find them and run tests. The only thing Cass doesn't know is why they want her.

She hides behind the vehicle, out of sight from her house in case the man is already out and coming for her, and grabs a penknife from one of her backpack's side pockets. She tries to stab it into the nearest wheel, but the blade won't catch. She grits her teeth, no time to try again and folds her blade back in and tucks it up her sleeve. She takes the break to pull on her shoes, too, then stands carefully and peeks around the van. Her hair is wet and plastered across her head which makes her skin prickle with discomfort and cold, and she has to blink rainwater out of her eyelashes to see properly.

"Got you," the man shouts, and Cass screams as he grabs her arm.

One of the windows of the Harris house at number seventy lights up, and Cass takes advantage of the man's distraction to wrench her arm out of his grip and sprint down the road as fast as she can. Her lungs, her head and her muscles are all screaming in protest and she feels sick because this is not in her routine.

"Demon girl!" The voice is a snarl right behind her and she tries to lunge away but he scoops her up around the waist, his grip locked tight no matter how much she writhes. As he carries her back to the van, she shakes her arm out and her knife falls into her palm. It opens with a flick of her nail and she slices at the nearest black cloth.

A yell and the man's grip slackens, but Cass only just wriggles out of his arms before they're back around her again and he's swearing, cursing her, his agency and the stars themselves. He calls her Cassiopeia and Cass frowns, but she can't tell him that he's got the wrong girl, wrong person. She's not Cassiopeia, she's just Cass, but she's also never been master over her own tongue.

He slings her into the back of the van and she tries to charge back out, but the door is shut and locked before she can throw herself at him, plunging the space into darkness. She throws herself down into a corner instead, and starts to count up in sevens until she can breathe again, then switches to running through a mental inventory. She pulls her backpack around to check that everything's inside, pulling the torch out first so she can see what else is in there.

The beam of light falls on a stack of papers already in the back of the van, and Cass frowns. The engine roars to life and she should be concerned about where she's being taken, but the pages are full of scribbles of equations and dates and notes. She recognises the date. Her birthday. Some of the notes are familiar, too: her father's name, the place he works as a scientific research assistant, and notes on herself. Her picture is pinned to a page headed by the name 'Cassiopeia', and there's a diagram drawn underneath, a constellation. 'Star Child' the man had called her; once all those years ago, and again tonight.

Cass stares.

The van goes over a bump that jolts Cass so she falls into the wall, but she doesn't sit up again. She thinks about the strange feeling in her limbs, thinks about what the man had said the first time he came for her. Her hands start to prickle. She goes further, thinks about what she'd read that the group believes about the meteorite baby, thinks about the pages in the corner of the van that date the meteorite to her birthday. The pins and needles spread to her feet and her calves.

In the front of the van, the man turns on the radio. Cass lets the rumble of the station add to the rumble of the engine and the rumble of the growing storm outside, all feeding into the buzz of her limbs. Everything gets hot and white and bright, and she has a moment to think that it feels fittingly like a supernova.

Then she explodes

*

A woman finds the remains of a van the next morning on her way to work.

"It looks like a bomb went off inside it," she tells the dispatcher, "but only affected the vehicle."

When the police arrive, they're baffled too. They find a gun, a bloodstained glove made of black leather, and a broken pink watch.

"The storm got pretty bad last night," the Detective Inspector suggests with a dissatisfied look. "Perhaps it was just a freak lightning strike."

"What about a falling star?" A new officer suggests, eyes bright and eager. The Detective Inspector makes a face.

"Peters, I highly doubt whatever happened here had anything to do with stars."

WISHBONE
Sebastian Bronson-Boddie

it is so nice to rest with you on the plum couch with the faded olive
cushions. or the hardbacked bench in the courtyard, every red clay stone steeped
in citrus. me with my arm draped across the back of it, wrist sitting
on the curve of your shoulder, natural. there, or sometimes on the slope
of your neck, pale and curved like a wishbone. the freckled
skin there is my favorite, dots of brown like drops of oil paint. my palm
knows your skin, too. they are lovers, lukewarm like the room
and the sangria we sipped earlier. but a whistle breaks me. it is the cardinal
reminding me. i am trespassing. it is hard to remember in these quivering
moments. easy, instead, to flirt and play
the fool. easy to forget time, and the sad sun, who is limping
towards the earth in clumsy half steps. it is time to go. the afternoon
has left without me.

CREDIBLE FEAR
Elizabeth Brown

A bare stage. Dusk. Lines indented with '-' are spoken from off-stage; voices in the night.

1. ANDRES, 9.

He enters the stage at a run, breathless. He stops in his tracks when he notices the audience, then looks back to where he has just run from, and back to the audience.

If *la poli* get you, they kill you.

- What?

The police. If they think you're part of a gang. Or smuggling drugs. Or anything. They kill you.

- How do you know?

I've seen them.

Beat.

Haven't you?

- No.

Really?

- Never.

You're lucky.

- I suppose.

What about the gangs?

- What about them?

You've never seen them kill anyone?

- I... no.

Wow.

A beat.

They don't care either, you know. Who it is they kill. And there's nothing you can do. If *mara salvatrucha* want you dead, you die. That's what my brother told me. It doesn't matter if you thought you were their friend.

So we're going to America. We're setting off tomorrow night, actually. Papi says there are lots of us who want to go, so we're going to go together. He says it's safer that way. And he says they can't ignore us when we get there if there are lots of us. His friend saved up all his money last year to get a car and drive to the border, but they sent him right back, and his rubbish little car broke down and he had to walk back the last 40 miles because he didn't have any money left to get it repaired.

We can't afford a car, so we're going to walk, and maybe try to hitchhike some of the way – I always wanted to do that, but Mama thinks it's too dangerous.

It's a long way, Papi says, but I don't mind. I like walking.

2. EMILIA, *16.*

She enters the stage, exhausted and weary, as the first two lines are spoken.

- We're going to stop here for the night.

- Donde estamos?

A beat. She takes in her surroundings.

Oaxaca, Southern Mexico. A town called Niltepec. The people are friendly here, they want to help. They meet us with soup, and medicine, and diapers and blankets for the children. They tell us *hola*. They tell us *bienvenido*. Welcome.

It's a warm night in Niltepec but the exhaustion from the day's walking and the fear of the night time keeps me trembling with cold. There are child-catchers around, they say. People have been following us, they say. Watching. Waiting. But Niltepec feels safe. The people smile at us and apologise that they can't give us more.

I want to take them by the shoulders and shake them. Their town is still in ruins from the earthquake – they can barely take care of their own! But they let us sleep there anyway. And they bring us their soup, and their medicine, and their blankets.

- I hope there are many more *Niltepecs* on the road to come.

Me too. Me too.

Beat.

- Where did you all come from?
- Where are you all going?

The world asks us. America, we tell them. Land of opportunity and freedom. Where we're from doesn't matter anymore.

- What will you do when you get there? They'll only send you back. It will all be for nothing.

We cannot think of that. We have already crossed two borders, and now we know that they can't ignore us when we reach the US. So, we must concentrate on surviving tonight.

The next morning, we leave, well before sun up. Somewhere along the road, two men walk up next to me, one holding a camera. The one with the camera says something in English to the other, who translates it in to Spanish.

- May we ask you some questions?

Who are you?

A moment while the taller man translates.

- We work for the American media.

He points to a large van behind us, gleaming white with big red letters on the side.

I've heard stories along the road. Of people who try to be your friend. Try to get you to trust them.

- Who are you travelling with?

My parents. And my older brothers.

- Where are you from?

San Pedro Sula, Honduras.

- And, why did your family decide to leave?

I study his face. Should I tell him?

- ABRE LA PUERTA!

- Quien esta ahi?

- ABRE LA PUERTA!

And before my father can reach the door, it is kicked open. Three tall men in balaclavas hold guns to his face. I stand behind him, wide-eyed. Terrified. They ask my father how old I am.

- Thirteen.

A lie.

- Cuantos años tienes?

The middle one asks, with a jerk of his chin in my direction.

Sixteen, I whisper.

- Eres muy guapa…

They walk in to the house, I stand there, in my night dress, trembling. They examine me. Stroke my hair. One puts a finger under my chin and tilts my head up to look him in his eyes. Cold, dark eyes which pierce through my skin and make me feel dirty. I try my best not to cry. The smallest of the three men nods. We'll be back for her tomorrow, he says to my father.

And then they leave.

Beat.

And so do we.

The man with the camera thanks me for telling him. There is pity in his eyes, but hope for us too. He stops and falls back in the procession of walkers to talk to some others further behind.

3. JOSEFA, *65.*

The lights come up on Josefa already on stage. She could be related to or travelling with Andres and or Emilia, but does not have to be.

A beat as she takes in the audience.

The US Border isn't really chain-link fence and men with guns and a Wall. In Tijuana, Northern Mexico, that's what you see. But that isn't the real border. The real border is made of paper. It's made of forms and men in suits and a language you don't really understand.

CREDIBLE FEAR

The border is a barrage of legal jargon and forty-eight hours to prove that to go back to Honduras is to die.

Except we can't prove it. I can't prove that I believe I'm going to be tortured or persecuted back home. The violence and the poverty and the fear isn't enough for those men in suits.

- So what will you do?

I don't know. *Credible Fear,* they call it. I must prove credible fear of persecution or torture for them to let me even try to claim asylum. Fear of being shot while buying bread or having my children not return home and finding their bodies hung in the street as a warning is not enough. Fear of starving to death is not enough.

- How scared is scared enough?

We have walked 4,453 kilometres, through Honduras, Guatemala, all of Mexico, and now here we are. And for what? For them to say no? Sorry, not good enough.

Find something else to be afraid of.

- How scared is scared enough?

I claim asylum.

I'm successful. They let me in. I settle a few miles outside of San Diego, just across the border.

- How scared is scared enough?

I claim asylum.

They don't let me in.

They send me and my family back to Honduras on a bus. We watch the thousands of miles we travelled on foot go by in a blur, in the opposite direction.

- How scared is scared enough?

I claim asylum.

They don't let me in.

I appeal.

I have to wait on the Mexican side of the border.

- On the Mexican side?

Yes.

For months we live in limbo. In an old leisure centre used as an overrun shelter while Immigration and Customs Enforcement consider my case.

- How scared is scared enough?

I claim asylum.

They –

Black out.

CHANGE HERE
Hannah Brown

"This is St James's Park. The next station is Victoria. Change here for the Circle and District lines, National Rail services, and Victoria Coach Station. This is the Victoria line train to Seven Sisters."

She hears this announcement every single day, it's so ingrained in her mind that she could probably recite it in her sleep. She walks like the hundreds of other zombified commuters on a Monday morning, barely watching her step as she takes her two trains: St James's Park to Victoria, Victoria to King's Cross St Pancras.

Every day, there and back. The same time every morning, and various times every night. Her life is always spent in some train station or another. And it's okay. Nothing special: just, OK.

Until that week.

Monday

She's lived in London for seven years, but this is the first time she's seen him.

" 'scuse me," he says, as they both step into the carriage, edging around her so he can hold on to the bar. He is about five inches taller, and his arm goes straight over her head. When he smiles down, she can smell the toothpaste on his breath. His teeth, though a little large, are nevertheless a stunning white.

She ducks her head to hide her blush and accidentally knocks the crown of her head against his jaw. "Sorry!" she cries, louder than she wants to as he reels backwards, his spare hand going to his chin. An old man behind her tuts.

"No worries," he says, and when he smiles a dimple appears in his right cheek. "Nothing broken, by the feel of it."

Giggling, she holds tighter to the bar above their heads, her knees becoming weaker by the second. Her train pulls up, and she's forced to get out.

Tuesday

"Hi," he greets her. This morning, he… greets her?

The second day of the week has already not gone well, and she's spent the majority of the wait on the platform trying to disguise a horrendous coffee stain she hadn't noticed when she'd hurriedly pulled on a shirt from the laundry bag that smelt sort of clean. At least, she thinks it's coffee. Could just as well be gravy.

"Hi," she responds, her stomach twisting. He smiles, shifting his weight inside his fancy shoes, the laces lopsided and a small scuff mark on the right toe.

"So-" he starts to say, but she never finds out the rest of the sentence. The train pulls up, bringing with it a great gust of air; she has to hold her skirt in place. The carriage is packed.

He motions for her to step on before him, but in the rush of people they are separated. He catches her eye before she gets off on the next stop, and smiles again. She decides that she will never get enough of his smiles.

Her morning continues on a little better.

Wednesday

Today is going considerably better than yesterday. She's even had time to pick up a coffee and manages to find a seat on the crowded platform. The train is late thanks to a delay somewhere beyond their station. She is engrossed in a Twitter spat between two people she doesn't know when she feels, rather than sees, someone sit beside her.

"Coffee?" he asks. She looks up and locks her phone with a tap of her finger, raising her eyebrow in question. He motions to her cup.

"Oh. Latte, no frills," she says, realising with a little disappointment that he's asking if she's drinking coffee now, not asking her on a date. "You?"

"Latte too, although I can always be persuaded to get a cappuccino. Have to get soy, though. Lactose intolerant." He shrugs.

"Oh," she replies, unsure of what else to say. She wants to follow it up with, "Where's your favourite place?" but the train pulls up and ruins their conversation.

Her kitten heels clack on the concrete. She stumbles, fumbling with the coffee cup, her handbag, and having to hold on as the train begins to move. A hand quickly cups her waist. "Sorry." Quickly removing his hand, he says, "I just didn't want to see you fall."

"No worries," she says. "I'm glad you'd rather catch me."

"Oh, I'm a gentleman, me," he jokes.

She smiles, and thanks him. She's about to ask his name but her interconnecting station lights up the carriage, and once again, she has to leave.

Thursday

She thought that Tuesday was bad. This morning, everything has gone wrong, and she speed walks onto the platform in a dirty bra with her unclean hair pulled into a messy bun to see her train pull away.

The handsome stranger – who doesn't really feel like a stranger anymore – is on the tube in their regular spot. Their eyes make contact for a split second before he disappears into the tunnel without her.

She waits for the next one, her heart feeling a little broken.

Friday

Today is the day. She knows that if she doesn't ask him out this morning, she never will.

She waits on the platform, even misses her regular 8:02 AM train to see if he will turn up. When he doesn't show – even though she looks up and down the platform nearly four times, and begins to get suspicious looks from fellow passengers – she gets onto the next train, the 8:07. Maybe they were never meant to be.

The doors shut behind her, then reopen with a "please mind the doors" message over the tannoy. She rolls her eyes, briefly presuming that a tourist has got their coat stuck before looking up, and there he is, holding onto her bar. Smiling at her. "Got stuck behind some slowcoaches," he says companionably, and she smiles, unable to keep a laugh escaping her lips.

"I'm glad you were able to catch it," she says. They pause, and she's working up the courage-

"Jonathan," he tells her, without being asked.

"Sarah," she replies as the train slows. Her hand moves to get a better grip on the bar, and their fingers overlap. "My stop," she says, filling the silence even though she's aware he knows.

"You work Saturdays?" he says, moments before the doors begin to shut with a whoosh.

"Mornings," she replies.

"See you then," he says, his voice carrying as the doors snap shut. He winks. It takes her a moment to step away from the platform, even after the train has entered the tunnel.

Saturday

She's ready for a rest. Her morning tube rides – just those special two minutes – make the days more bearable, but she's still looking forward to a decent lie-in.

He's waiting for her at the platform and hands her a coffee cup. "Latte," he says. "No frills." She takes it from him in a surprise, thanks him, smiles, then looks at his jeans.

"Interesting choice of a suit," she says, and they step into the carriage together.

"Oh," he says, as they take up their respective handholds on the bar, "I don't work on Saturdays."

He gets off the tube with her at the next station. "Do you work Sundays?" he says, winking.

"No," she replies. "Thank God."

He laughs. "Good. Would you, um, like to go to dinner with me tomorrow?" His cheeks flush, and he bites his lip.

She thinks about it, for a millisecond. "I would love to."

"Fantastic," he says. He passes her a slip of paper. "I figure you have somewhere to be right now so I wrote down my number. Text me later, if you're still up for it." She takes it and slips the paper into her pocket. She'd text him now if it were possible to get phone service on the damn London Underground.

"I'll see you tomorrow, then, I hope." He smiles, turns around as the next train comes in, and gets on it. She waves to him through the window.

Sunday

They meet on the platform, but this time she's wearing flats and a dress that stops above her knees. He's wearing a shirt, but to her relief has paired it with jeans. She wasn't sure quite how formal to go.

"Where are we going?" he asks, and she smiles.

"I found us a place. It's just two stops."

"How mysterious."

They take the tube in a silence that seems both awkward and comfortable, filled with little smiles to each other. He moves his hand forward, seemingly nonchalant on the handrail, and it brushes against hers.

On the platform, they scan their cards and she leads him up the escalator. Her friends know the restaurant she's chosen, just in case, but even when she texts them that she's there, she feels no reason to worry, already comfortable in his presence. Nerves still tangle her stomach, but she feels a flash of excitement skip through her heart too.

The escalator bends and they step off. She turns back to him, smiles, and they both take a deep lungful of fresh, cool air.

BROKEN BUBBLE GUM MACHINE
Amelia Court

She can't move her fingers. They're as brittle as ice. Again & again & again & again & again & again she twists her wrists to thaw & shift the block. She can't type or write or even take a sip of water can't even take a sip of water to swallow the painkiller. It's pointless. It won't help it won't help this time. She's stuck like that hairband in her head that won't stop looping around her pulled back hair it won't stop looping again & again & again & again & again & again & again never getting any tighter, still too loose to hold the hair in place. A twitching is starting a twitching is starting in the back of her jaw jolting like her mind is trying to break out of her body's shell, twitching & tugging at the muscle to bend the bars it's built around itself. These gates are closed for the night. She swings as she sits she swings & swings one leg until the tock tick tock ticking scuff scuff of her shoe forms iambic beats her chest reflects each pound. Every passing hour drains another drop drip drop of blood from her skull, they drip down her spine in spirals like marbles cascading down a bubble gum machine. Her brain is soon sapped dry, dry rot spreads outwards black & sticky it sticks her cells together. She's hit a wall so hard her teeth have fallen out & scattered on the concrete scattered white spots like catch-lights watching her from the wet black concrete. If she had tried a little harder it wouldn't have happened, if she tried a little harder she'd be able to move her fingers, if she could try a little harder the hairband would stop looping again & again & again & again & again & again. Now it's tightening around her wrists cutting the blood flow. She can't move her fingers. They're as brittle as ice. Again & again & again & again & again & again &

WYRM
Grace Curtis

"Hey Josie." Wayde whispered.

"Hey Josie. Hey Josie."

Josie kept eating, trying to ignore him. On the floor, Laura giggled. She had two horses, one in her hand that she was making hop about between the tiles, the other submerged in her mouth up to the shoulder.

"Laura, petal, don't eat that –"

While Mam was distracted, Wayde kicked Josie under the table, slamming his toe into her kneecap hard enough to make her spit out her cheerios.

"Ewww!" he shrieked. "Mam, Josie's eating with her mouth open!"

"Play nice, you two." she said, buttoning Laura into a cardigan. Josie shifted her chair out of range. "Have you got plans today, Josie?" asked Mam. She nodded. "Playing with Henry again." She did a crinkly eye smile.

"That's nice. Keep an eye on her, okay Wayde?"

He grunted, leaning in so she could kiss his cheek. "Lunch is in the fridge. I'll see you later." Mam hauled Laura into the air and backwards out the door. The moment the latch clicked shut Josie bolted from her seat, grabbing her back pack from under the table. Wayde caught her by the elbow.

"Off to see your little friend again?" he sneered.

Josie yanked her arm free.

"Go away."

"When are you gonna invite him round, hmm?' he asked. 'I've been dying to meet your *totally real* –" She slammed the back door, cutting him off.

*

Henry was already there when she arrived, perched on a lichen covered boulder in the corner of the car park. "Good morning." he said, hopping off. "Have you got the supplies?"

"Uh huh."

Josie emptied her bag – an apple, a banana, two Kit Kats, and a cereal bar – and watched as Henry ate them all in the space of a minute. It was amazing how much he could eat for such a skinny boy. "Excellent," he said, wiping crumbs away. "Alright then, squire. On our way."

Josie trotted after him.

"What's squire mean?" she asked.

"An apprentice Knight," he said. "I teach you what I know. You bring supplies and help me out with things. Get it?" He looked at her, wary for a moment. Afraid she'd argue.

Josie nodded. "Okay." she said. "I'm a squire and you're a Knight."

"That's right." he said, flashing a smile.

"Come along, squire." Emboldened, he started to walk even faster, and she nearly had to jog to keep up with him.

"A Knight has many duties."

As he spoke his voice became posher, firmer.

"It's not all killing monsters. Upkeep. We maintain the harmony of the forest. Look here –"

He stopped abruptly, nearly making Josie bump into him. Right by the path there was an oak tree, the bark scarred roughly with overlapping shapes and letters.

"Brownie markings. See?"

He traced his fingers along the lines. "Fresh, too. They leave these here as coded messages to each other."

Josie gazed up at them, "What'd they mean?"

Henry dusted his fingers off. "Nothing to worry about," he said. "Just marking territory. Might be a good idea to pick up any rubbish you see, though. Stay on their good side. Brownies don't mind people hanging around, but they hate litter. They find it ugly."

They walked on in fits and starts, Josie stopping to grab cans and crisp packets and throwing them all in her bag. Henry didn't talk all the time, but she liked that. The silence made her feel calm. At the end of the day, when they were parting ways in the car park, Henry told her she'd made a good start.

"I ought to test you properly, though." he said. "You gotta be brave if you really wanna be a Knight."

"I'm brave!" Josie protested.

"Mam said so."

Henry gave her an appraising look.

"We'll see. Tomorrow. Bring extra supplies."

*

The sacred tree was deep within the forest, growing atop a little mound in a thicket of evergreens. Under a green sheath the long branches pinwheeled away into the sky, converging in a knotted point right at the base of the clouds. Looking up turned her stomach like she was looking over a ledge.

"Do I really have to go up there?" Josie asked. "Henry...?"

Henry had already started to climb, slinging himself easily from branch to branch. Josie realised the only prospect that scared her more than climbing the tree was being left alone on the ground.

"Wait for me!" she called.

Painfully, awkwardly, she pulled herself up one branch, then another. Then she glanced down. "Henry!" she called upwards. "I'm scared. I can't –"

"It's okay."

She couldn't see where he was, but his voice called down, sanguine as ever.

"Close your eyes. Take three deep breaths."

Josie hugged the branch against her chest and tried to breathe.

In-out.

Too fast. She forced herself to slow down.

In, out.

Not so bad. She tried again.

In.

Out.

The world calmed.

"Better?" he asked.

"...Yeah."

"That's an old Elven trick."

The tree jostled as he kept on climbing. "They're great hunters."

Eventually – after hauling herself with shaking hands and scrabbling feet, higher and higher, after the ground had dropped away almost to nothing – Josie caught up with Henry. He was sat on one long branch, his arms resting on another, his chin nestled in the crook of his elbow.

Josie stopped, following his gaze. At first it was too dense to see, but then she noticed – there was a gap in the thinning branches, a blue-green portal to the world outside. An ocean of rustling treetops spread out beneath them, peaked and rounded like a city skyline. Her eyes went wide.

Distracted, she wobbled, and put a hand down on his shoulder. Henry jumped away like he'd been bitten.

"Sorry!"

"It's okay." he muttered. "Watch your footing."

Gingerly, her knuckles still white from clinging on, Josie slipped into a seat next to Henry. She glanced over to him. He looked distant.

"Um..." she cleared her throat. "Did I pass?"

"Oh, yeah," He waved one hand. "You're brave enough. For sure."

"Phew."

They hung there for a bit, legs swinging into nothing.

"Is it scary then?" Josie asked. "Being a Knight?"

Henry nodded.

"They hate me," he said. "Monsters. I get attacked a lot. Even when I'm sleeping, sometimes."

"Really? I have nightmares but they can't get me after I wake up, it's only dreams and that."

"Yeah." He pulled at his cuffs. "They hate me a lot."

Wind breathed through the leaves.

"Probably because you're such a good Knight," Josie said.

"Probably they're scared of you."

Henry smiled. "Yeah."

Another pause. Then he hauled himself up. "Alright," he said. "Time's wasting. You ready for some more lessons, squire?"

Josie beamed. "Yeah!"

Time warped like cheap plastic in the heat of summer. Josie's world became sensory, moving between fragments of feeling which spiked in her mind like a seismograph – the smell of burnt toast first thing in the morning; evening sky the colour of strawberry ice cream; Henry's eyes, grey ringed, scanning the matted earth for mushrooms. Home was worse and better. Worse, because Henry had shown her how desperately boring her life was. Better, because she knew that she could escape. Wayde's kicks, Laura's screams, shrill, grating music from the TV; all of it passed. None of it mattered. The forest was waiting.

*

There came a day at the height of summer, dreamy with sunshine, when Henry declared, stuffing the last of a Coco Pops Bar into his mouth, that they were going to the holiest place in the entire forest. He was cheerful that day, and whistled as they walked down a diminishing track towards a grassy clearing. In the centre of a clearing was a circle of rocks, rough-hewn, almost as tall as Josie. She thought at first they were a pile, but getting closer she saw that they encircled something. A hole in the earth.

"This is the well of ancients," said Henry, placing one hand on the rocks. "It's the centre of the whole forest."

Josie went to peek over the edge. "Careful, squire," he called. "Even I don't know how deep it goes."

There was a wink in his voice – an out of character cheekiness. Josie shrugged. "Uh huh. I know." Ever so slowly, she poked her head over the edge. It was too dark to see past a few metres, but she thought she could hear something – a distant hum, or a rush, like the inside of a seashell.

It smelled like rainwater.

"Henry." She looked up at him, hands still on the edge. "How do you become a Knight?"

A faint smile appeared on his lips. "You have to kill a monster."

"So you – you've killed one?"

He nodded. "Uh-huh."

She stood bolt upright. "Can I hear about it? Please?"

Henry paused, looking into the well. "Sure. I think you're ready now." They sat down on a couple stones, Josie with her legs crossed and her back straight like she was in class.

Henry shifted himself into a comfortable position, and then switched into his storytelling mode – deeper voice, more hand gestures.

"You know how to tell when there's a monster in town?" he asked.

"The first thing you notice." In a slight motion, Josie shook her head.

"It's easy. Monsters are famous for terrorizing villages, of course, but a new monster won't start there." He grinned wickedly. "It always starts with the children."

*

"Hey, Josie!"

The Coke can bounced off Josie's ear, splattering lukewarm liquid down her shoulder. She kept her eyes on the ground as a chorus of laughter went up. They were gathered on the other side of the street, a nameless jumble of boys, agitated, bored. It seemed like every summer there were a few more of them. Wayde was the leader.

"Where you going, Josie?" one cooed.

"Off to see your friend?"

"Don't *fucking* ignore me!"

Wayde's friends were like dogs – they chased you if you ran. She kept her legs stiff and slow, shuffling like a zombie round the corner and all the way down to the high street. Only when she saw the tree line nudging out between the terraced shop fronts on the edge of town did she let herself break out into a run.

When she arrived, Henry didn't ask why she was panting. He didn't speak much at all as they walked down the trail that led to the bay. It was September, and the leaves were turning into little treasure maps overhead.

"Um," Josie broke the silence. 'Are we gonna fish again today?'

Henry nodded, his eyes ahead. They fished with a pasta sauce jar Josie stole from home, taking it in turns to stand in the river holding it against the current. Henry had never explicitly said what they were fishing for – just to hold the jar steady, and watch out.

Josie was first to go. Normally Henry would tell stories while they fished, but today he just paced around the bay, nudging pebbles with his toes.

"Anything?" he called. She shook her head.

He kicked his shoes off and waded in next to her, scrutinizing the jar. It was empty. Brown water gurgled at the rim. Impatiently, he grabbed the jar and pushed it further in. Josie held on, startled. Their hands were touching, but Henry wasn't jumping or pulling away. She thought maybe he hadn't noticed.

"Come on," He muttered. His eyes were locked on the river.

"Come on."

Upstream – a flash of something black. Josie had just registered it when Henry wrenched the jar upwards. "Squire!" he yelled. "Lid!"

Josie fished the lid out of her pocket, and Henry screwed it on tight. He exhaled.

"Got it."

He held it up, letting light filter through. Inside – just visible amidst the muddy water and tufts of moss – there was something alive. A limbless black creature about the size of a finger, thrusting its body against the smooth surface of the glass.

Josie stared. "What is it?" she whispered.

Henry smiled. "A monster."

MINDFLOW
Alice Davies

Winter Garden

in this winter garden
the sunflowers wilt,
holes dug into soil
for seeds that will never grow.
you can't see the rain
but the ground is flooded
and the light is shining
on a different patch.
how about
that –
a garden that doesn't
suit this time of season
there's no reason
a winter garden
can't grow.
but here it doesn't
and maybe one day
you'll see the rain
and the sun will fall
in just the right place.

Notes of The Night

sometimes the ground opens up
and I fall.
unexpectedly.
hands clawing at the soil
soul
and feet hanging
in the air
heart hanging
down the stair.
it's a cold night to be
out right now.
music rain
shattering the ear
I'll hang by the
note.
maybe the ground
can't take me
if I live on a sheet of music.
I'm flying away -

I'm flying away with the tune.

Shut Out

I wonder what those eyes are saying
I wonder what those eyes are saying
to be praying
hands SHUT like the door
eyes fallen to the floor
I wonder what those eyes are saying
I wonder what those eyes are saying
I saw them praying
but now I'm
shut out
eyes that hide yet
SHOUT
I stare at the door handle
shut staring at the
shouting door handle

Mirroring Waters

the sky waters.
a blank slate
creating
unseen reflections
my eyes
water in
oblivion.
—
oblivion.
water in
my eyes
unseen reflections
creating
a blank slate
the sky waters.

COMPETITION
Dylan Davies

Lucy was only fourteen when she went to hospital,
Bangles around her swollen elbows,
Her calves tapping at the tips like knitting needles.
I watched her leave, knock-kneed,
Jeans bunched over four layers of leggings;
Her joints seemed to bulge and swell
At the edges of her skin
Like bulbs from freshly stirred compost,
Like foreign objects begging to be removed.

When she was gone, her absence thrummed in the air
At thirty beats per minute,
Warning us of her heavy eyes,
The winding saline and electrolyte drips
(We, young and imaginative,
Held down bile at the image,
Thick globules of intravenous invasion),
The eyes on her bare, fugu-sharp body
Round the bathroom door,
The unsteady thump of night time alarm clocks
She might not wake to.

We lived in the gaps between her blood tests,
Her potassium count like commas tallying my missed meals,
A staccato of semi-colons to our thrown away pack lunches,
Screaming out, in desperate palpitations, to the bins
Where we dumped out brown bread sandwiches.
Her bones, marrow wasted,
Pierced, without sterilisation,
The fleshiest parts of me.

COMPETITION

Days eked past, dripped unwillingly into our veins,
Until March gave me nausea and fifteen candles,
A raw and aching celebration;
She couldn't be there,
Still chained by NG tubing to her wheelchair,
But she mailed her gift to me,
Artwork borne from hours of
Food Relationship Art Therapy:
A picture frame, black cardboard and
Infant school splatterings of glitter.
I put my face in her design and
Marvelled at the newfound chasms of my sunken face,
The plummeting cliff-edge of cheekbone -
How small I felt, knowing
She was not.

I told her I wanted to give her my blood,
My bones, my marrow,
My steady, consistent heart,
Wanted to turn my unwilling body into her charity,
My guilty abundances of flesh into
Dainty rivulets of girl-kindness,
Wanted to give it all to her
In organ-sized packages;
But really
I longed to gouge the fat from myself,
To whisper through rotted teeth bedtime stories of
Scalpels and needles and liposuction,
To bury her in my silhouette's heaping excess,
A suffocation of weight,
Until I was light and free and useful, while
Lucy could no longer breathe and
Dreamed of me.

OTHER: A short one-woman play
Ella Dorman-Gajic

There is one woman onstage. She plays both WOMAN 1 and WOMAN 2. Dialogue in speech marks indicates that the characters are talking to each other.

WOMAN 1

> I've always found it very awkward, the process of knocking at a door and waiting for someone to answer Especially if you have never met that person before.
>
> You try to figure out where to stand; what expression to pull; how to place your hands.
>
> And half-way through fussing over your blouse, the door opens. Revealing a woman. Her.
>
> Or, at least, I think it's her.
>
> I notice she has a crease between her nose and left eyebrow. The exact same one as mine. For a moment, I see me.
>
> I smile.
>
> I say hello in her language. One that I'm desperately trying to force back to the surface; it's like squeezing myself back into a former skin, one that I shed many years ago. That part of me feels like a dying light bulb, softly drifting in and out of focus; dimly flickering on, then off.
>
> An echo of a smile traces across her lips and she nods her head. Suddenly, I have vanished.
>
> I wonder who she pictured waiting behind this door?
> A foreigner. A refugee. An immigrant. A British woman. A businesswoman.
>
> I wonder which identity fits best with who she sees before her now.

I am all of these things. And yet, in this moment, I am none of them. I am only the unfamiliar face looking back at her.

A stranger.

She gestures for me to come inside. I realise this is the first home I have been in since coming to this country. Coming back to this country, I should say. There is an unfamiliar aroma in the air; maybe it's a form of spice. She leads me through a tiny kitchen. I notice almost all of the cab- inet doors have fallen off their hinges, but this is nothing. Some of the houses I passed in this neighbourhood are skeletons, half-standing upon a foundation of rubble.

She leads me into the living room and invites me to sit on her single sofa. I look around. Cracks seep out of the corners of the room, leading to a cluster of little brown holes, like an army of ants. The top layer of wall has broken away, revealing the brick work underneath. The only thing on display is a beaded wall hanging, holding a large pendant with a symbol and words on I don't understand.

I try to break the ice. I tell her I have been in the country for a week. I've been trying to find her.

WOMAN 2

'A week is not so long. You knew my name. Yes?'

WOMAN 1

'Er... yes. But I didn't know you were -'
I pause. Try to find the language.

'I only discovered you were here... just this year. And they gave me your old name... before you were married.'

I know I am getting this all wrong. I look at the crease deepen above her nose. Mirroring mine.

'They told me you had died, years before. With them.'

WOMAN 2

'With them?'

WOMAN 1

>'With… our parents. When I was told they died, they said their baby did too.'

>I say these words just as I had rehearsed them, night after night. I needed to get them right. She needed to understand.

WOMAN 2

>'I was ill. From her injuries. And the pollution. They thought I would die.'

WOMAN 1

>'But you didn't.'

WOMAN 2

>'Well… no. I am alive.'

WOMAN 1

>'Yes. Of course.'

>I try to smile this off. Make a connection. But her face doesn't change. It's concrete.

>I notice she hasn't offered me any food or drink.

>I think back to the first time I was in a stranger's house. I remember it feeling very warm, in comparison to the outside air. And so full of stuff. Paintings. Nick-nacks. Food. Steaming food, cooked in ways I had never seen before. A glazed chicken glistening through the steam of fog.
>Brown, runny sludge in a weirdly shaped vessel. A pile of little golden hills that looked like their insides had been scooped out.
>'Yorkshire puddings' the stranger tells me. 'They're my favourite.' Then I remember when I brought my first school friend home with me.

>The stranger, now my mother, had made us little finger jam sandwiches with orange squash and we played Mario Kart on my new Nintendo Wii. For dinner she made us spaghetti bolognese with garlic bread, then apple crumble with custard for dessert. Mum's food was always the best, but it was even better when I brought friends round. She liked to make people feel at home.

I think of my childhood. The cups of tea, the Victoria sponge, the football matches, the muddy trainers, the ironed shirts, the Lurpak butter, the scented candles, the piano, the open fire, the Christmas presents.

And now I'm back here. I see this country. I see this woman, who has had none of the things I did.

'I didn't want to leave her.'

WOMAN 2

'She sent you alone. Her child. Why would she do that?'

WOMAN 1

'She had to stay.'

WOMAN 2

'There was no reason for her to.'

WOMAN 1

'I know. I didn't want... please believe that. I wouldn't of wanted... I mean, she was part of the revolt. She would have been caught if she fled.'

I remember her kissing my forehead. Telling me to be brave. I was digging my fingers into her back. Clinging to her. Shaking. I had been screaming all day. The itchy scarf she had given me was now completely damp. I was four years old. I didn't want a new family. A new country. A new life. No matter how much our house trembled, or how many times she'd read me bedtime stories against the sound of gunshots, or how many of our friends' homes had turned to gaping holes. I wanted to stay. I clung to her like I was clinging to the edge of a cliff, as if she was the only thing left keeping me from drowning.

But as I pressed my cheek against her belly, I was also pressing into the person growing inside her - the woman sat in front of me now. Just a wall of flesh between us. If she'd known that, then maybe it would have been different.

WOMAN 2

'Did you get a new family?'

WOMAN 1

'Yes. Erm. The people, who helped me, they… erm.'

WOMAN 2

'They adopted you?'

WOMAN 1

'Yes.'

WOMAN 2

'Do you have a job?'

WOMAN 1

'I'm in business… I help with running it. How about you?'

WOMAN 2

'No. My husband works. In a shop.'

WOMAN 1

I watch her play with the thread of her scarf. It's just like the one our mother gave me before I left. The only thing I still have of hers.

'I would like to help you.'

WOMAN 2

'I don't need any help. That's not why I agreed to meet you.'

WOMAN 1

'No, I know that. But I… excuse me, I…'

My words lose touch with each other on my tongue. I look at the bare lightbulb on the ceiling. It's starting to softly drift in and out of focus; dimly flickering on, then off. Is that in my head?

WOMAN 2

'Yes?'

WOMAN 1

'Money. I... I have it. I can help you.'

WOMAN 2

> 'I have my own money. I can take care of myself. The life that you lead has nothing to do with me.'

WOMAN 1

> 'But you are my sister, I want to help.'

WOMAN 2

> 'Just because we share the same blood.'

WOMAN 1

> 'You're the only real family I have.'
> She goes silent. Glances down at my clothes. My jeans, my polka-dot blouse, my new heeled ankle boots.
>
> I open my bag.
>
> 'Please... let me give you something.'

WOMAN 2

> 'No. Don't.'

WOMAN 1

> 'It can be a gift.'

WOMAN 2

> 'Stop. I don't want you to pity me. Do you think, just because you come from England, where there is no war, where you have wealth, where they tell you that we are the poor people - that means you owe me something? You don't. This country was rich once, too. Many people here still are.'

WOMAN 1

> 'I'm sorry. I didn't mean to offend you. I only want to get to know you.'

WOMAN 2

> 'Money will not make you know me.'

WOMAN 1

> 'Yes.'

WOMAN 2

> 'I would've given anything to have known you. To understand you. To understand how you did it. How you managed to get away so easily.'

WOMAN 1

> 'Did you not try to leave?'

WOMAN 2

> 'I couldn't get a passport... My birth certificate was destroyed in the hospital. And anyway, I wouldn't have taken that risk. So many boats have gone missing. Or sunk, in the middle of the ocean. Lives wasted, for nothing. My friends, my neighbours... even ones who have reached the borders were stuck there, waiting to get in. For months. I couldn't do that.'

WOMAN 1

> 'But I could help you get a passport. We could prove you are my sister. You could even come to England, with me. If that's what you want.'

WOMAN 2

> 'No. I couldn't leave my home. I'm married. And what would be the point? The war's over. I survived. Look, my husband will be home soon. He doesn't know you are here. I said this would only be a quick meeting.'

WOMAN 1

> 'Would I not be able to meet him?'

WOMAN 2

> 'I haven't warned him. He doesn't like surprises.'

WOMAN 1

> 'But will I be able to see you again?'

WOMAN 2

> 'Yes. Maybe.

Pause.

Can I just ask you, before you go. What were they like?'

WOMAN 1

'They were…'

The bulb stops flickering. The words appear before me.

'They were kind. I hated them for sending me away. Alone. Then I spent so long feeling guilty, that I didn't deserve the luck I'd been given. To be alive whilst they were dead. But they believed in what was right. They fought for it. And they trusted in the goodness of others. Trusted in the goodness of the people who took me in. Somehow, they knew I would be alright.'

We nod our goodbyes.

And I am outside again. I look back at the door that divided us. Look back at the stomach I clung to. And I think of myself: the same height, the same eyes, the same crease. I see myself stripping off the skin I could have lived in.

THERE'S NO 'I' IN 'DENIAL'
Milo Filtness

"Right, that's the beef wellington in the oven. Everything else is ready to go and I just have to bung it in later. All I have to do now is check that the possets are setting." Jon's wife Karen pours herself a large glass of Merlot. Jon himself sits at the breakfast bar reading the news on his iPad. "It should be good fun, I think Penny might even be bringing Scattergories."

"Oh good," Jon said.

"I hope there's enough wine for everyone," she opens the fridge to check. "That's enough wine, right Jon?"

Jon looks up without moving his head. There are ten bottles. "For eight people? Might just stretch."

"Oh, no! There are ten of us now. Very last minute - I forgot to tell you, I invited the Astons!"

Jon's head jerks up. "The-the tennis club Astons?"

"No, the ones we met in Dorset at the pottery class! Would you believe it - turns out they're staying with friends in Sevenoaks for a few days, so they're popping down for the evening! I thought it would be nice to catch up with them - isn't that exciting!" Karen's face is positively alive, whilst Jon's eyes are buzzing like radio static.

Jon manages to squeak out a laugh, "Ha! What a coincidence – amazing!"

Karen stares off and sips her wine, letting out a 'hmmm' as she deliberates. "It must be just under a year since we've seen them face to face – no, over a year! Obviously I ring Suzanne all the time, she's such a love, she was telling me the other day about a discounted chaise lounge she found in HomeSense…"

Jon isn't listening – he just nods along to Karen's story, punctuating with the odd 'oh!' and 'uh huh!'. He cannot believe this is happening. What the fuck is he supposed to do? Can't fucking believe it. Is there any way he can leave? Anything to avoid the Astons. Fuck. Fuck fuck fuck fuck…

"Jon! Only eighty pounds for a chaise lounge, Jon! Eighty pounds! You do find some really good stuff in there – like that little bedside table I got for Maisie's room, except she wrote 'poo' all over it. I was distraught." She tuts into her empty glass of wine.

"Five year olds." She goes to pour more Merlot. Jon puts down his iPad and slightly too casually hops down off his stool.

"Very good, K, um, I just need to pop down to Waitrose."

"No you don't – what for? Have I forgotten something for this evening?" Karen's brow is furrowed and her mind is running, double checking if she bought garlic for her dauphinoise potatoes.

"No, no, just…um…thinking about it, ten bottles of wine probably isn't enough. Especially now the Astons are coming, because I know Suzanne drinks rosé."

Karen is aghast. "Oh shit, of course! Oh god, that could have been disastrous! Yes, go go go! But take the Jag in case I need to pop out." Jon matches her next utterance word for word in his head –

"I can't drive that bloody thing, it's like a tank." She says it every time someone mentions the car.

"Okay, K. I won't be long."

He grabs his keys and hurtles for the door, leaving Karen bustling around the kitchen collecting things for the dishwasher.

*

Jon makes it to Waitrose in four and a half minutes – record time. He finds a nice parking spot with other spaces either side and reverses in. Once parked, he turns off the car, his straight face collapses, and he starts to cry. He sobs and sobs, leaning his head on the top of the steering wheel and letting his tears fall onto his knees. His limbs are loose and his heart feels bludgeoned. He feels as if he's about to vomit his heart up. He opens the car door and just vomits his lunch up instead. He moans and sits as still and helpless as a February morning.

His heart screams.

Ever since he last saw David, Jon awakes in the ocean of his bed, barely afloat, waiting to feel a bit better – he wakes up every morning with the hope that he will, and every morning when he asks himself how he's feeling, the answer is always 'worse'.

Every day he misses David more.

The first time he saw David, Jon noticed how perfectly ironed his shirt was. They sat next to each other and joked about their wives dragging them to a ceramics class, then talked throughout the whole thing. The plates they made were terrible. Jon and David went for dinner that evening whilst their wives went to a wine bar. They discussed their morning commutes, how they have their steak, and if either of them had managed to get Wimbledon tickets this year. They were together for hours as they both tried to figure out why the conversation was flowing so easily. They snuck back to their sleeping wives in the early hours of the morning.

The last time he saw David was three months ago – they met in Reading as it was halfway between the two of them. They had told their wives they were on a work golfing trip. They had spoken about how wrong their feelings for each other were and how the sneaking around had to stop. It wasn't fair on their wives. This was the last time. They then cried and kissed and fucked. They held each other all night in a hotel bed.

The next morning David had left by the time Jon awoke. He left no note. He didn't even accidentally leave a sock that Jon could keep as a memento. He even took all the free toiletries from the bathroom. Jon cried into his continental breakfast in the middle of the hotel dining room.

He is snatched out of his reminiscing when an old lady knocks on the car window. Her glasses are wonky.

"Are you alright? Do you need me to get some help?"

Jon does not know what to do with his hands, he straightens his back, and weakly smiles.

"Oh! Um, yes…I'm fine thank you, just came over a bit funny. I feel okay now, thank you." He continues reassuring the old lady until she trots away, dragging her Bag For Life behind her.

Jon thinks about a joke Graham Norton told on Radio Two this morning – "There's no 'I' in 'Denial". It's a stupid joke that made no impression on him at the time, but now its silliness seems very comforting. He lets himself chuckle. He repeats the joke in his head as he pulls on composure like a jumper and gets out of the car, making sure to step over his sick.

*

Back at home, he puts the rosé in the fridge, and heads upstairs. He can hear Josh shouting in his room. He peaks round the door to see his son with a headset on playing on his Xbox.

"Everything alright in here?" He smiles as Josh whips round.

"Yeah, when's dinner? Do we have to eat with everyone else?" Josh asks as he takes off his headset. Jon is taken aback at how chatty he's being.

"No, you've lucked out, you and Maisie are having spag bol. I'll do it in a minute. Are you hungry then?"

"Yeah, kinda." He puts his headset back on. His chattiness is short-lived.

"I'll call you when it's ready." Josh grunts in reply. With that, Jon closes the door.

He goes into his bedroom – Karen is sat at her dressing table in a new dress (bought for the occasion) putting on her makeup. His stomach deflates. She notices him and smiles in the mirror.

"You took a while – was it busy?"

Jon walks over and kisses her on the head. "Rammed."

"Oh well, at least you're back now. I guess it is a Saturday." She stops patting in her concealer and looks at Jon. "Why are you looking at me like that?"

"No, no… you just look really pretty." They smile at each other with warm eyes.

"You're so sweet sometimes." They chuckle. "Now, I need your advice – do I attempt a smoky eye? Or will it be too much with my dress?"

"Every time you do a smoky eye you say it makes you look like a whore and you wipe it off."

"Oh dear. You are *very* right." Karen is giggling and her cheeks are blushing. "I'll just use my gold one."

She continues giggling at her lack of makeup skills and forages through her makeup bag – Jon notices she has the tag still on her dress, picks up some nail scissors from the dressing table, tells her to hold still, and cuts it off.

"I'd better go do the kids their dinner, then it'll give me time to give the kitchen a wipe down before everyone arrives."

"Thank you, darling. I'm nearly ready." She's still giggling as Jon walks away in pain, thinking about how much he loves his silly, silly wife.

*

"Helen! My darling, come in! Oh, and you've brought *canapés*! And Michael! So lovely to see you – have you lost weight?" Karen does the greetings and cheek-kissing as Jon gathers coats and various plates of hors d'oeuvres. He hears about the Dalton's trip to "a lovely village just outside of Beziers," the Smiths regale him with the issues they've been having with their bathroom renovation, and Andrew Collins grumbles about how next door have put 'Vote Labour' signs outside their house – "it really lowers the tone of the cul-de-sac." Jon feels a bit sick.

He excuses himself to the kitchen to check the carrots are roasting, but instead stands over the sink in the downstairs toilet, gripping the side. Everyone is here except the Astons. He can hear everyone hubbling and bubbling outside and all he can think about is walking out the front door and not stopping. He looks at himself in the mirror and sees greying hair, ruddy cheeks, and a dirty secret behind red and itchy eyes. He's so tired and in love and confused. He's not gay – he loves his wife and kids, and still (even after sixteen years of marriage) gets unbearably horny when she wears her red lacy underwear. They still have sex at least thrice a fortnight and she reminds him of a Saturday night in front of the TV with a packet of chocolate buttons. He loves her despite the fact she rambles on and on, and prides herself too much on the fact she shops at Waitrose.

But he wakes up in the morning with David on his mind, and he knows (even though he doesn't remember it) that David has been in his dreams as well.

"OH MY GOD, SUZANNE, MY DARLING! AND DAVID! I can't believe it!" Karen's voice barges under the door.

Fuck.

Jon feels sick again. He knows he can't hide in the bathroom any longer as Karen will be *dying* to reunite the four of them, and will probably whack out the wobbly plates and mugs they made in their pottery workshop for everyone to laugh at.

He looks himself in the eyes in the mirror.

He's not gay. He's definitely not gay. He loves his wife and kids.

He is not gay.

He's got this.

He feels sick, but he can't stay in the toilet all night.

Jon is just going to have to put on his composure jumper once again, laugh at his pottery skills, and make pleasant small talk with David about his stay in Sevenoaks. He has made it through the last three months despite being in a constant state of veiled taboo and despair, so he can do this.

He thinks again about Graham Norton's joke from this morning and takes solace in its simplicity. With that in mind, he opens the door and steps into the fire.

MIDAS, NO LONGER KING
Francesca Finch

This is the Golden Age.
All you have fought to accomplish
All your blood you have spilled
And drained, all you almost died for.
It's before you in heaps of fool's gold
In charcoal and jewellery and the stray
Gems and emeralds scattered in between
What you thought you wanted and what
You got.

There is malleable metal in your hand.
It bends to the imprint of your palm
And you would have killed for this.
You have wrought and reaped
Hoarded anything that caught the light,
Any glitter or promise of riches
You wanted this, and the Gods will not
Allow you to forget that.

This is the Golden Age.
Your viper touch has left your lover
Nothing but a weeping angel at your throne,
Poisoned and beautiful and glimmering,
Gold in the light, she is casting an ethereal
Radiance across the palace hall and her wrists
Are decorated with cheap regalia.
She wears trinket rings and you have placed
A plastic crown on her gold dead head.

You are wading through water
With your hands full of greed and coated

MIDAS, NO LONGER KING

In blood, you are caked with metal stains,
Green and bronze patterns on your skin
Where the paint wore off and the
Illusion faded away
And your body recoiled under the weight
Of your avarice.

This is the Golden Age.
Your pockets are weighing you down
Against the river and the Gods
Are unsure if you have come to repent
Or to bargain but they will take no
Less than your life and don't you remember?
This is what you wanted.
You would have killed for this.
You cannot repent for the blood you wasted.

A barrage of water knocks you over and
Devours your crown first, before
Seeping into your thick, expensive tunic,
You are waterlogged, and you are selling
Your tears for your lover's life but you
Are not ready to die because you would not die
For what you thought you wanted,
Only for what you thought you were promised.

This is the Golden Age.
You are purple and gold and soaking.
Your strength against the current is
Waning and there are no gods
To save you now, only there to watch you drown,
And the pennies you carried are floating
Around you and you want to scream
Into the cold air because how dare they
Take your Golden Age away from you.

Jessica Firman

The embodiment of possibility, potential, promise,
anticipation, expectation, determination,
generation after generation encompassed.
You epitomise us all.

EGG

Jessica Firman

You're gospel. Omniscient.
Alone, I seek your guidance,
treasure your answer,
surrender to your judgement.
Never shall I question you, as others do.
Never shall I worship others.
Never shall I waver.

WIKIPEDIA

WITHOUT WATER
Willa Froy

David: "I needed to get out, it smelt like dried mud."

Her: "Like Uncle?"

David: "Maybe"

The funeral had been warm, and dust scented. We'd stood in a circle, as Uncle's grave was lowered in. The box was grey partridge coloured with little gold lines that coiled round and laced him in a bodice of decomposition. Mum said we'd see him again and crossed her fingers over her like grandma did. Then they had left me there, even David - they knew Uncle would have wanted me alone to talk. My mouth was sandpaper and the words pricked needles over my tongue and pierced my throat; I spat out the sour bile.

Everyone met later in our house, but David said he needed to get out of there.

David: "I feel a bit mixed up at the moment, I think I'm multiples of myself, I need to explain that to you"

Her: "Mum liked seeing you, everyone likes to see you, they must meet someone"

David: "yeah, but. Listen. but. You don't see it"

My Uncle could shoot an animal and look right into his eyes with a conviction I admired and despised; raise the gun at one of his one-pound bargain hunters and pull the trigger without a shadow of a tear along his lower eyelid. The horses had a breath that seemed like ours, searched for a freedom in the same way.

We were down by the bottom river about to do some bush burning when we heard blood being drawn out from something. It was a squeal that rocked your heart into the middle of your throat. A rabbit had got caught up in a wire in the top field, wrapped around his head and cut into the sockets of his eyes. Uncle could shoot him too.

For blindness, he said, made life not worth living.

David: "I wish you'd stop"

Her: "Loving you?"

David: "Trying to comfort me, trying to make me happy and smile, you're just not really capable of it"

I had met David sat on the stairs of my neighbour's house when I used to live with Uncle. I had crept over again, so I didn't have to listen to shouts for a bit. I'd sit on the ridged feet of the back door, just to breath slow. He said he "caught my hair above the window", said it waved right at him.

A voice that wasn't mine had entered my head and it felt like the milk in the glass bottles. David's stories raced up the grass hills and fell into my innocence at a pace that consumed. How he went to Italy just to see what was there and found nothing but a jug of fairly delicious cream. He'd smelt perfumed India and held the hand of a life-crushed man who bled out his armpit from a war wound that never stayed closed. He'd licked the dried salt from Lake Mono when it crusted dry upon his parted lips. I found it easy to fit into his jigsaw shaped shadow, and that pleased me enough to try cement its borders.

David: "You're so plain, so quiet, I can't be both of us anymore, it's too much pressure for me, especially now"

Her: "I don't think, I…

David "How are you so fine that I see you like that, that everyone sees you like that"

I remember how I stood at the edge of the stage at school, as smoke sprayed into the one nostril not stuffed with hair chemicals, and overheard a girl say behind the black curtain that green "wasn't right" on me and my hair looked like "electric therapy they did on mental people".

My voice jutted just below audibility, below the sea level where life bubbles are frozen immovable. All I saw was Uncle's watery smile from the crowd which rose to meet his cloud high frowns.

David: "I can be two separate people at times"

Her: "I could love two as one, a hundred as one"

David: "I know you do"

Uncle could talk as if a person really listened. Sit down in a room as though his body was before the furniture. Shout at the woman in the car park even though she didn't really do anything wrong. The shouts tasted stronger than cider vinegar and he didn't "give a fuck" who choked on it.

David: "You should stop though"

Her: "With you?"

Him: "I think that's what I'm telling you, in an, I love you way, in an, I need you way."

Lip wrapped around lip till they confused which one was on top of the other. I hid behind the back of a wooden fence and watched their hands interlink to be a turned loop of knotted wool. I didn't know then that a kiss could make you bored, that it didn't always turn your feet to a liquid that poured into the centre of the earth.

They looked half frightened of what their bodies knew to do. I saw the way their hands followed the hair line to their necks. The push of their hips as they wrapped into one another. His arm round her back looked like it could replace her spine. It looked safer than sleeping with a pillow on your chest.

David: "I'm simplifying it all for you and you're still okay with silence with not saying anything at all"

Her: "I know you never tell me everything, you don't really have to"

David: "You're the one who never talks"

At school the teacher taught us how to toss a stone and hop. We didn't understand the rules, but our feet had a daggered black lens that spotted the chalked lines before our heads did. We drank in that we could play the game without the need to listen.

David: "How can you love both of me?"

Her: "I think you over complicate yourself"

David: "We're a confusion"

I had wanted to dance on hot coals, jump high into toe curled smoke. Then melt into a puddle David could jump into.

David: "You are so fine with this, that's kind of weird you know, it's like you don't even care"

Her: "It's not weird"

David: "I love that you never see the difference"

Uncle took me to a shoot, we stood by the other hole entrance. Waited. The terrier barked hot air down the other, I watched Uncle raise the gun. Green bodied, with a circle mouth that spoke into the ground, that taunted. His finger with desensitised breath, waited, on the trigger for his command. Uncle's eyes narrowed, he pushed his body closer, and smelt the marshy entrance. His cap hid his face, but I knew exactly what it looked like, as if it had been stewed in red wine over a low flame.

After the shot ran out, I cried into my shoulder behind the stump of a tree that got cut last year. My hand's a sample sized flagstone blanket I hid behind. Whispered a happy thought, a happy dream. I tasted on the side of my wrist sea tears, that bled out quicker than blood.

David: "You know… I'd never…I never did all that, what they were saying I did"

Her: "I know, it's me"

David: "Just a bit, you should take responsibility, go tell them"

David was like an upside-down boat on the grassy ridge of a beach that only harbours freckled stones. He was both old and new, with hands that where rougher than the rope that had found its way from the sea and dried unbendable.

David: "I could just stay here a little longer"

Her: "Yes, if you want."

David: "Exactly, if I want"

Once my Uncle kicked my left knee. Shoved his foot against my skin laughed and ran upstairs. The force toppled me over, I lay still for a little bit, imagined I had drowned and how guilty he would feel. But it wasn't bad, and it didn't hurt. When he stopped the fights, we never touched at all. I remember my purple laces had undone, I could have fallen on them, I must have.

David: "But, I get so angry around you"

Her: "Even now, here? I'm sorry"

David: "I forgive you every time, it's not your fault you don't understand me"

We used to have breakfast for dinner, only when all we had was milk. I loved going to sleep in a reverse. Sat at the high-top table and let the cereal soften to a paste that slipped down my throat soft as sea weed that makes you forget about the sand. Stare at the sky and wonder where the clouds would go next, if they wondered the same about us. The spoon in my little hand reminded me I was a child, with the hammered sterling silver of unpredictable.

David: "I'm going to go soon, go do something by myself for a bit"

Her: "I guess. I…"

David: "It's not up to you, I can't think about you all the time"

I wish our first kiss had been different. Not so strong and fast. David's tongue was a spade which dug at the roof of my mouth. When we stopped to breathe, I took a peak at his eyes, the way they mixed from sea mist to grey, but they looked entirely different. He pulled me and took my mouth with his. I had wondered what he would taste like and his hand gliding down. I'd forgotten about his fingers that crawled.

David: "I used to think you were someone else"

Her: "I don't think I mind that I'm not anymore"

David: "That you've disappointed me"

We had been in silence round Uncle's dugout pit. I watched them pour dirt over him, prayed he would dig his way out to heaven. I became the river mouth of goodbyes, and I spoke to blank faces with the clarity of sea salt. When the mound was finished, I didn't know where to put my eyes. David said I could sit in the chair that he was in, next to the hunchback tree. I sat. But at once begged him to take the seat, I swore would turn me bruised. My ears were angry at my head. I stood. I felt the water in my chest slip out of me and slide under my bare feet, the death had made me float, just me.

David: "We've been doing this for too long"

Her: "Yes"
David: "I'm bored of your incompleteness"

I used to believe I could read Uncle's thoughts. Recognise the connection between face and mind. I was a rock carved out by his waves and I knew the exact shape he wanted, like folded napkins on the table or the scent of lavender in the bathroom. His hand in mine a balloon close to burst, mine a fleshy heart which tried to disguise itself in feathers.

David: "It's not all me, you're not what everyone sees"

Her: "No I'm not"

David: "You're so confident in your pretences"

Last week when Uncle was in hospital I went, without David, and danced on my own in the place we used to go to when we thought we could make friends through beer bottles. A girl I knew was sat outside with someone who had similar hair on the sticky stone steps. We'd spoken about stuff which made me notice how clear the air was, how it spilled into my lungs in awkward silences, in between the little laughs and jolty daydreams. Funny how when the stars appear, we could return smiles. I saw the same girl from that night, walked crossed armed. Yet when our feet tap along the pavement and a smell of sun honeyed grass washed our faces, we're silent as empty airplanes. I was okay with no conversation, I liked it.

David: "I'm going to go"

After everyone left our house with Uncle shaped memories and the ability to forget, I went for a swim. The water fell onto me, goose bumped my skin numb. I held my hands together, thumb interlinking thumb. The salt water wrapped me in its bitter fluid, till I flowed and moved like a fish. I heard what I told David repeat and repeat like the churned-up waves. The ocean swell pushed and moulded me. I was whatever the sea wanted me to be and nodded as its whispers slipped into my ears, it smelt safe, more than anyone ever did.

Her: "I want you to go"

THE BATTLE FOR BRITAIN
Sam Gardham

Harry Batter, agent of Her Majesty's Secret Service, was escorted into a long dining room by two armed henchmen. They stood aside and Batter noticed a sinister-looking middle-aged man sitting at the other end of the table: Stefano Bratavank, his arch-nemesis. Arranged around Bratavank on the table was a great banquet. His bald head looked up from eating.

"Death is an acquired taste, Mr Batter." He dabbed at his mouth with the napkin tucked into his collar. "But the chicken is good, too. Would you say it is a taste we share, you and I?"

"The chicken? Well, I must confess a liking for coq au vin in a particularly rich sauce."

Bratavank sighed. "Come come, Mr Batter. It is not as if you are unfamiliar with the subject of which I speak. Like myself you are sustained by the act of *killing*. And so…" He grinned. He really was very European. He spread his arms wide. "Let this great feast of mine sustain you too."

Bratavank clapped and a waiter set out a bowl of coq au vin for Batter at his end of the table. He went to sit.

"Don't worry, Mr Batter, it's not poisoned. I have brought you here to ask you something, not to kill you."

"And what's that?" Batter tucked into the coq au vin. It was pretty good.

Bratavank sat back in his chair, forming a steeple with his hands. He watched Batter over it. "Why did Great Britain vote to leave the European Union?"

"You mean why did we vote to leave the Alliance of Nations Unbearably Smug?" Bratavank looked shocked.

"Oh yes," Batter continued, "we've known for years that your ANUS organisation is behind the EU. And we know Europe is conspiring to weaken us economically, introducing all this silly food with unpronounceable names into Tesco and so on. Well, no more. The tables have turned, Bratavank. Or, should I say..." Batter raised an eyebrow. "...The dishes."

Bratavank choked and clutched at his throat, knocking his bowl and cutlery clatteringly off the table. "You English dog!" he growled.

Batter sipped at the 1952 Pinot Grigio. "All your staff here are in the employment of Her Majesty's government. Although, I must say, they didn't have to poison your food much. I know you're allergic to various kinds of condiments."

Bratavank collapsed forward onto the table, dead.

Winton Sacheverille, head of MI6, came in through the double doors. "Excellent job, Batter. Hopefully we'll be able to blow soft Brexit wide open now. The state of play couldn't be clearer."

"I'm not sure it's as clear as all that, sir." Batter walked over to where Bratavank's head was slumped on the table. He grabbed it by the hair and pulled - the mask came off.

"Dear god," Sacheverille said. "It's Jeremy Corbyn!"

"I noticed during our discussion that he was wearing a mask. Bratavank must have been Corbyn all along."

"It certainly makes sense. I did find it suspicious that he was in favour of national nuclear disarmament. He spoke Spanish as well, didn't he?"

"Yes, he did," Batter said gravely. "We should have known. There's no telling how many members of the Labour Party his ANUS has turned to the path of evil."

"Well, you've done a sterling job, Harry. The nation is indebted to you. Now, you've just reminded me about your next assignment–"

At that moment Jeremy Corbyn drew himself back up into a sitting position. He pointed a gun at the men and cackled, sneering evilly. "Gentlemen, I survived not winning a large-enough majority - I can certainly survive death."

But before he could fire Batter snatched a chicken leg from his bowl and launched it spinning through the air like a boomerang. It smacked into Jeremy Corbyn's gun, knocking it to the floor. Corbyn looked between Batter and his empty hand with his mouth open in amazement. Sacheverille drew his gun.

"Now, I just wanted to say you've got it all wrong," said Jeremy Corbyn. "I was trying to revive our nation's economy, not damage it."

"I'm afraid that doesn't make sense," Batter said. "You're too left-wing."

"Actually, come to think of it, you're right. It doesn't make sense." Jeremy Corbyn scratched his chin and looked pensively towards the ceiling. "Perhaps I've been wrong about everything all my life." He stood. "There can only be one kind of government."

"The Conservatives!" they all said, turning to face the wall of cameras and microphones on the far side of the room.

"And cut!"

Theresa May clipped excitedly towards them from behind a camera. "Excellent job, boys!" She rubbed her hands together in glee. "This will be a *wonderful* advert for the party. Jeremy, I can't thank you enough."

Jeremy Corbyn nodded meekly and blushed.

"Oh, it was nothing, T. Now, since I've done you this favour, perhaps you could consider… Oh, I don't know." He shrugged. "Dinner, perhaps? And afterwards, maybe…" His voice squeaked: "A coalition?"

Theresa May smiled warmly. "As it happens, Jeremy, I think that's what my husband said to me on our wedding night. He was never a smooth talker, you know." Then her eyes narrowed to slits. "But he didn't end up getting what he wanted either."

"Oh."

She spat at his feet and stalked off. "Alright, chaps. Well, thanks again,'" she called over her shoulder jubilantly. "I'll go and give Boris a ring now. He's going to be just *thrilled*. Byeee!"

The actors who played Harry Batter and Winton Sacheverille sighed and shrugged their coats on. "Bye, Jeremy."

"What? Oh, bye." Corbyn was gazing into space.

He turned and watched them walk off through the doors towards the bare walls and lighting scaffolds beyond. Then his eyes darted around, checking no one else was still on-set. As often happened in distressing situations, he had a sudden craving to give a lip sync performance of 'I Will Survive' by Gloria Gaynor.

But Jeremy Corbyn hesitated. Surely the political life of Great Britain didn't involve musical numbers? That would make it all look too farcical, too Harry Batter-like… But wasn't it farcical? David Cameron had called for the EU Referendum and resigned after the result.

Remembering this suddenly made Jeremy feel free. Alone in the room, he put the song on his phone, climbed up on the dining room table and lip synced spiritedly with his eyes closed. He pulled all the disco dance moves.

THEATRE
Kasper Hassett

A long, metallic lift engulfs two
Lights sedately amble through it.
Having dropped, it hums and ponders
Before reopening an incision for escape.

Backstage is half abandoned.
You follow the Theatre Blues
To a room sick of seats.
You take one; the rest are your audience.

Alone, the seats lose their scorn, and spectres
Of closed curtains linger.
They share your gown, only
Hearts are stitched to the sleeves of theirs.

Sterility seeps in like a smokescreen; conceals all
And you are beckoned by stagehands.
"Are you the star of the show?"
"Are you allergic to stage fright?"

The theatre's secret hub of scrubs
Invites you to a publicised slumber
In a haze, applause brings you under.
You didn't see the curtains raise.

STUDY OF MICHELLE
Maya Hayes

You're walking down the corridor. Your stride is purposeful. You know exactly where you're going, even if you're not quite sure what you're going to do when you get there. You just want to look at it, you think. Just a little look. Just to check.

You start to feel sick.

The floor tiles are slick under your ridiculous skyscraper work shoes and you stumble slightly, the frictionless drag between pointed heel and polished marble. Your lips are crudely painted red and your face is pale and bloodless. Almost there. You wipe your sweaty hands on your sensible pencil skirt. A few scattered tourists murmur around you, some covertly snapping photographs of the more famous sculptures and canvases, but your presence goes unnoticed. Then you see it.

You stare at the painting for a long moment. You take another step, then another, and then you're nose to nose with The Lover's Rose, or: Study of Michelle. You look into your own smiling face on the canvas, and you feel so terribly sorry for her that it's overwhelming.

You lean forward the infinitesimal distance between you and yourself, tottering on your stupid heels, and kiss her forehead.

Then there is a shocked gasp, and silence, and then a lot of panicked shouting. *What's all the fuss about?*

*

"My client maintains, Your Honour, that this was an act driven by selfishness, bitterness and momentary insanity. The mark itself bears no artistic significance and indeed lends no secondary merit to the piece itself. Might I remind Your Honour that my client spent upwards of three years completing this piece from conception to completion, and for this effort to be seen matched by an act of sudden jealousy from the defendant is nothing short of defamatory."

The barrister steps back with a self-satisfied nod and the courtroom is silent for a moment. There is a lot of nodding, some hushed words of agreement. What a selfish thing for someone to do.

The painting is in front of the courtroom, the poised body of the defendant arched in a coy profile. Her bare back is turned as she tosses a playful glance over her shoulder, and a single red rose is within her slim fingers. Then, like a mark of Cain, the red lipstick stain pressed firmly to her forehead. The perfect imprint of a kiss.

*

There is a party, of course. A party to celebrate his wonderful achievement.

"You must be very proud of him, Michelle. You must be so very proud!"

There are so many people. You don't know most of them- there are a lot of art critics, of course, and obscenely rich gallery owners, and there are his friends, most of whom you've never even met before. He's told you before how he likes to compartmentalise his social groups. Makes it easier, he says, I have to be so many different people in life. But how many of those people do you know? In marrying your husband, how many other men did you marry?

"In a way," your husband declares to cackles from the crowd, "it's Michelle's party too. There can't be a *Study of Michelle* without a Michelle! Seriously though guys, I couldn't have done it without her. Couldn't ask for a better muse."

Everyone is smiling indulgently at you. You laugh, self-conscious. Your likeness is burned into the psyche of everyone here, but it doesn't belong to you anymore. You are no longer the curator of your own image.

You feel like you're looking at yourself through a broken window, and you decide to step outside to get some air. Your garden feels foreign and strange. The wooden patio furniture you picked out so carefully looks cheap and childish now. Party guests are perched delicately on the edge of the chairs to avoid crumpling their silk gowns. Everyone is talking and laughing, but you can't seem to remember how to speak at all. After a couple of shuddering deep breaths, you turn to go back into the house and see your husband with another woman. She is much younger than you, and he is kissing her neck.

In the few seconds it takes your role to switch from devoted wife and muse to cast-aside harridan, you sweep into the house and lock yourself in the bathroom.

*

"The psychological damage, Your Honour, wrought upon my client by being victim to the prosecution's infidelity is paramount to my case. Indeed, it is my belief she would be perfectly within her rights to demand distribution of the painting be immediately ceased, on the grounds that her image is being profited upon by her ex-husband without her consent. However, this is not the case. My client wishes only that the uptick in interest and reflected price be rightfully shared with her. Intended or not, this painting is now a collaborative piece, and my client wishes to split the value of the painting accordingly."

There is an incredulous intake of breath from the prosecution. "A collaborative piece how? She defaced it! She had no right-"

The judge dismisses him, and the court is adjourned for the day. As everyone files out, the estranged pair catch each other's eye. He opens his mouth for a second, then closes it and looks away.

*

Your moment of insanity has repercussions far outweighing your expectations. You're surprised by how much everyone cares about this painting- you think perhaps a little callously that it was never very good in the first place. It was a good likeness, certainly, but it never really felt like it meant anything. It seems, however, that a great many important people disagree with you.

What is really surprising, however, is that some of those important people are very excited about your 'addition' to the piece. Everyone wants to know about the girl who ruined the painting. A story is spun of dramatic tensions, a marriage filled with suspicion and infidelity, a husband who broke his wife's heart and the vengeance she took on his magnum opus in response. It's partly true. There was an infidelity, a heartbreak, a woman left confused and desperate and alone. The only thing wrong is the motive. You've tried to explain to so many people that you weren't angry. Not in that moment, anyway. You just felt so sad and so sorry for yourself, sorry for the girl in the painting who didn't know what had already happened to her. But sadness isn't as marketable as the jealous rage of a scorned woman, and nobody is listening to you anyway.

The story starts to pick up more and more speed. Art critics are getting involved, the question of money is being raised, and suddenly you are in the house you left weeks ago, and your husband is screaming at you. *Don't you realise what you've done?* His reputation, he tells you, is in tatters, and it's all your fault. *Why didn't you think about me for a second, you selfish bitch?*

This is the righteous anger they were looking for. This is what it feels like, to be angry and in pain and lash out like a wounded animal. You feel it now, and it consumes you.

The next day, you begin the process of a legal copyright battle with your own husband. It feels like a suitably petty thing for this new scorned woman to be doing.

*

Was the party where everything went sour? It's hard to work out when you knew how this would end. The party seems right, it's an easy starting point when you're explaining yourself in a courtroom. Seeing your husband entwined with the curator of the gallery where the portrait of you was proudly displayed. But you weren't shocked when you saw them together. When did you know that you had already lost him?

If you think about it, if you track it back to the moment you truly realised, you find yourself at the memory of sitting for the *Study*. Not the first time, of course- that was new and exciting and full of the promise of your new marriage. You were both wrapped up in it, infatuated like children.

The moment things changed was two years later, one of the last times you sat for the painting. It was in its final stages but there was still important detail work to be done, and nothing seemed amiss for a long while except-

Except when you looked at him you realised he wasn't looking at you at all. And when he turned the canvas around, the woman staring at you had none of the wrinkles around your mouth or the freckles on your back. It wasn't really you he was painting any more.

That was when you knew.

*

At night, and when it's not needed in court as evidence, the painting returns to its home at the gallery where this melodrama started to unfold. In the daytime it's guarded more carefully now; nobody wants another would-be artist putting their stamp on it and making the situation even more complicated. In the evening, though, when the gallery is closed, security isn't so severe. If you're the right person with the right kind of contacts, it's easy to find your way into the gallery for a midnight viewing of the artwork.

This is how you both find each other. He walks in to find you sat in front of the painting, this symbol of everything you've put each other through.

"Why are you here, Michelle." It's not a question. He doesn't sound particularly surprised. There's a cold disgusted edge to his voice that makes you wince.

"I wasn't doing anything."

There is a brief uncomfortable silence. Then he explodes.

"You make me fucking sick. I can't believe you're here after everything you did! Do you even understand what you destroyed? All of my credibility as an artist is fucked now because I'm attached to some stupid gossip story for middle aged women to talk about! Everything I built up is gone because of you, you're so bloody pathetic!"

You don't respond.

"Have you got *nothing* to say for yourself? You're not even going to apologise? You're not even going to try and defend yourself? Was this all just an elaborate ploy to piss me off? Because it's fucking working, Michelle, I swear to god!"

"Aren't you going to apologise to me?"

He stops.

"What?"

You turn around for the first time. 'Aren't you going to apologise for what you did?'

He rubs a hand over his face and laughs incredulously. "God, you have no fucking clue, do you? This is so much bigger than our relationship, can't you see that?"

Something snaps inside you. You've never been a violent person, but you want more than anything to break your knuckles on his jaw. He's angry, but he isn't in pain, and your sudden desire to see him hurt overwhelms you. Instead of approaching him, though, you walk towards the painting. You rip it off the wall and before he can speak you stamp on it, your heel piercing the canvas. You don't stop until mud distorts the picture and the canvas is ripped beyond any repair.

He's frozen in shock. Then he chokes out, "What the hell have you done?"

You look up from your mangled likeness and blink, dazed. Then you start to laugh.

FAITH
Judith Howe

I have never really known how to pray.
Face lifted to the old beams arching to the heavens,
the smooth wood craning upward.
I'd think about the construction of the church,
or that Great Truth:
so many of the most beautiful buildings we have
are built of religious text and sweat,
and blind hope, acknowledging that we are all
stumbling around in the dark.
But when the sun begins to sink into the horizon,
leaving behind streaks of what has been
in shades of a sky set alight, and the stones
clatter into each other like the only song
we've ever known, and something new
being birthed into existence just here,
lingering in these few seconds,
with the waves hushing all thoughts of human skill,
culture and invention away.
A murmuration of starlings dancing in the lingering light,
and the iron husk of the pier standing testament
to decay, this bare exoskeleton witnessing the crumbling
of the sheen we paint over fleeting achievements.
Here, I think I understand.

A DAY AT THE BEACH
David Hubbard

In the sea.

"Mummy says I can't go past those rocks."

"But that's where the crabs live!"

"Well I don't like crabs."

"Baby."

"I'm not a baby!"

"You are."

"I'm not."

The sea made her feet hurt. It was too cold.

"I want to go back."

"But we haven't got a crab yet."

"I don't want a silly crab. I'm hungry. My mummy said I can have breakfast here."

"My mummy said I can go anywhere on the beach."

"No, she didn't."

"Yes, she did. And I want a crab."

He ran away. She didn't. He came back with a baby crab.

"Look!"

"That's yucky. Put it back."

"It's wiggling!" he cried.

"Put it back! My mummy says you shouldn't touch yucky things."

"My daddy says he ate a crab once."

"Eugh!"

"He said it was yummy."

> The crab didn't look yummy.

"Put it back."

"No."

"Put it back. I don't like it."

"I do like it."

"Well, I don't."

"What's his name?"

"It could be a girl!" she said.

"No, it couldn't. It's too strong."

> He poked the crab.

"You're being silly," she said.

"He's called Mr Tickle."

"You can't call him that."

"Why not?"

"He doesn't look like Mr Tickle."

"He's got funny long arms."

"Put him back."

"I'll put him back if you hold him."

> She didn't want to hold him.

"You're being silly."

"You're being a baby."

"I'm not."

"You are. Only a baby would be scared of Mr Tickle."

"I am not scared of Mr Tickle."

"Then hold him."

"What if he bites me?"

"Crabs don't bite, silly."

"Fine."

She held Mr Tickle. He wiggled.

"There."

"See? You were being a baby."

"I'm still hungry. Go and put him back."

He grabbed Mr Tickle. Mr Tickle pinched his finger. He started crying.

"He won't let go!"

"Stop being a baby."

"I'm not!"

She pulled Mr Tickle off his finger and threw him into the sea.

"Stop crying."

"I'm going to my mummy."

"I told you to put him back."

"Well I don't listen to stupid girls!"

He ran away. She shouted at him.

"You have to be nice to me if we're gonna be friends, you know!"

*

On the beach.

"I don't like all these silly little kids on our beach. They're too noisy."

"I think they're cute."

He scowled and stuck his hands in his pockets.

"They cry too much."

She was a couple of steps behind him as they walked.

He didn't like the way the sand was scratching between his toes.

"Why are you being so moody?"

"I'm not."

"You are. What's wrong?"

"I don't like beaches."

"You used to."

"Yeah, well I don't anymore. Only here because mum made me come."

"You mean you didn't want to see me?"

His cheeks felt hot.

"I didn't know you'd be here."

He thought he saw her smiling out of the corner of his eye. His cheeks grew hotter.

"Well, why don't we do something together to cheer you up?"

"I don't—"

"Oh come on, it'll be fun!"

"Like what?"

She skipped in front of him and blocked his path.

"We could go swimming?"

"I don't have my trunks."

That was a lie.

"You could roll up your trousers."

"No."

"Okay then, why don't we go exploring together?"

"Just me and you?"

"Yeah."

"No. I think I'll just stay here."

"And be sad?"

He didn't say anything. He couldn't look at her so he looked out across the water instead.

"Why are you being so weird around me?"

He didn't answer.

"You don't have a crush on me do you?"

"Of course I don't."

He started walking again. She didn't follow this time.

*

On the cliff.

"I'm getting the train back up next Friday."

"Already?"

"Already."

She ran her hands through the grass and watched the wind ruffle his hair. It felt like he'd only just come home.

"I thought the summer holidays only went fast when we were kids."

"Me too."

Laughter drifted up towards them from the beach below.

"We should do something before you leave."

"Like what?"

"Have a party?"

"I have enough parties at Uni."

"You told me you don't go out much."

"I don't. You know how much I hate it."

"Well, what do you want to do instead then?"

He didn't say anything for a while.

"Everyone spends too much time thinking about the future. How about we just enjoy what we've got? Just enjoy this?"

"This is pretty good."

She put her head against his chest and closed her eyes. She'd expected his heartbeat to be deep and slow but it was pounding. She looked up at him. "Are you okay?"

He was fiddling with something in his coat pocket.

"Yeah, all good."

"Is there something you want to tell me?"

"Something I want to ask you."

She watched him take his hand out of his pocket. A boat drifted lazily along the horizon.

"But it can wait."

*

By the café.

"Sun's going down soon."

"Mm."

"Paper says the tide'll be out."

"Uh-huh."

She didn't look up from her phone. He sat there watching her for a moment. Her cup of tea must have gone completely cold by now. He tapped his ring finger against the table listening to the clicking sound of metal on wood.

"I was thinking of buying a Rolls Royce."

"Yeah, sure."

"Great, I'll put it on your credit card if that's okay."

"Uh-huh."

"What's your PIN again?"

"Sorry?"

She finally looked up from her phone. He just gave her a tired smile.

"Don't worry about it."

"Look, honey, I'm sorry. It's just you know how work can be.

Every time I reply to one email two more appear."

"No, it's fine."

"It isn't."

"No. Maybe it isn't. But that's okay. You keep replying to them."

"You know what?"

She threw her phone into her handbag and sat up straight.

"No more phone for me."

He smiled at her, properly this time. She took a sip of her tea and looked at the cup guiltily.

"Am I really that bad?" she said.

"I'll buy you a new one."

"No, it's fine. This can be my punishment."

Neither of them spoke for a few minutes as she sipped the cold tea. A few cars rumbled past, each full of shrivelled children and sunburnt parents. He watched each one of them as they drove up the country lane.

"You remember when we used to spend all day at the beach?"

"Until the moon came out and it was just the two of us."

"That was good."

"It was bloody chilly."

He laughed.

"We were younger then."

"Yeah. We were."

The sky was turning pink. He looked back across the table at her.

"We should go again."

"What, now?"

"Yeah why not? All the families have gone home."

"They've gone home because it's time to go home. We should be off too, we've still got to get food for tomorrow. I was thinking of doing a casserole but…"

She tailed off. He was tapping his ring on the table again. A waitress came and cleared away their empty cups. She waited for the waitress to leave before speaking again.

"You were being serious?"

"It's fine."

"You want to go down to the beach."

"Don't worry about it."

She got up from the table and went to the car. He sat there watching the sunset on his own. Something hit him on the back of the head.

It was a towel.

He looked up.

She was running down the lane laughing.

He took off after her.

*

At home.

She was standing by the window when he came into the kitchen.

"Whatcha looking at?" he asked.

"Red sky at night."

"Hm?"

"Nothing, dear."

"You gotta speak up, darling."

"Maybe if you put in your hearing aids for once."

She smiled at him so he knew she wasn't angry.

"Maybe if I did. For once," he said.

She looked back out of the window.

"It looks so peaceful from up here."

"All you can do is see it from up here. Can't hear it. Or smell it, or taste it. That's prob'ly why it's so peaceful."

"No. I think it's peaceful because it thinks no one's watching it anymore."

"What was that?" he asked.

"Never mind."

"You want a drink?"

"No, I'm fine thanks."

He made himself busy, leaving her to watch the last sliver of light disappear into the water. Her cheeks felt wet.

"How many more do you think we get?" she asked.

He didn't answer for a long time.

"That ain't up to us now, is it?"

"No. I suppose it isn't."

He finished making his cup of tea and set it down on the counter.

"Do you want to go down to the beach tomorrow?"

She nodded but didn't say anything.

"Way I see it, you can't ever be too sad about a sunset," he said.

"And why's that?"

He joined her at the window, chin resting on her shoulder, fingers laced over her stomach.

"Because for someone out there, it's the first time they ever seen one."

Then he tickled her until the tea went cold.

SITTING TIGHT
Joe Hull

Sitting tight in a thin seat, my bubble shuts out the sound.

Shimmering and shaking in the air around me, it hangs, a firm and dusty film, pulsating gently with my breath, dulling the shapes of the people outside.

I try to speak, just to see, and a soap bubble drifts up from my throat, coming to rest at the top of my enclosure and bobbing there gently until it pops. Someone glances at my face, and I wonder if it was one of those bubbles that sounds like a word.

I look down at the hands in my lap. Wan, bony skin and scum-tucked nails; they don't look like my hands. I look at the ceiling, and allow myself a breath, slow and deep...

Too deep.

The bubble inches forward, sucked in with the air, tightening and tugging at the precious space around me. *You'd better be careful.* I shift my weight gingerly and look around at the faces outside. They're all acting like everything's normal.

The air's getting stifling and hot as my exhalations make their tight circuit and return. I slow down. Inhale, more gently this time, and hold it. I close my eyes and the bus goes dark, but human beings aren't like other animals – we don't need to open our eyes to see the things that frighten us. I try hard to forget about my hot, plastic prison. *Don't look. Don't look.* I try to think about the world outside, and how many beautiful things there are. Ancient, cobbled streets where I've never smelt the fresh bread; cool, misty ravines where I've never shielded my eyes from the sun; cocktail bars on the beach with dancing fires and dreadlocked girls. But that's all out there, and I'm in here. I could go and see those places, but I'd still be me; I'd still be inside.

I feel my eyes come open.

You have to breathe.

My lungs lurch and start and I let in a gasp of air. A couple of people are eyeing me, wary, and the bubble squeezes itself tighter once more. *Not here. Not now.* It's inches from my lips and when I breathe in I can feel its thick, choking edge, bubbling between my lips. I rub my face like I'm trying to get dirt off it.

Resist.

But it's so close now and it's happening, it's coming for me.

Don't breathe...

I cast my eyes around, desperate. Blurred, far-away faces floating in the shimmering air. I can feel hot fingers brushing my shoulders and I know I shouldn't breathe but when I don't breathe it makes my heart jump and when it thumps like this my thoughts go black and now they're racing tracing dark patterns all leaping and chanting and grinding themselves together –

Let it in.

Like a drowning man, I take one last gasping breath, deep and desperate, and the film drags in and tightens its heavy fingers over my body. My open mouth poured full of hot plastic gunk that sticks in my throat and suffocates me with its toxic smut. My fingers clawing at bare arms, lungs gulping and gasping against the deluge, the poisoned fabric of the bubble needling at my nerve endings, delivering its viscous mass of harrowing sounds and traumatising shapes. A scratched record that's skipping again and again, the repeated segment condensing each time and growing in volume until it forms a single roaring wall of panic, each second a pulsating singularity of fear and choking breath...

I look up. Everyone is definitely looking now. I wonder what the whole process must look like to them. *Them*, clutching their bags protectively on their laps. *Them*, with their sinkhole mouths and their silent, staring eyes.

I can breathe again now, and when I breathe I breathe but I breathe only soap, and every word I speak is a hot sick-bubble hacked out from a burning chest; I can see again, but my eyes are covered over with a thin mist. After something like that, it's like the world's all been placed farther away. The bubble's pulled itself in, it's enveloped everything I was, and my whole self feels numb. At least things are quiet now.

I get off at the next stop. No-one looks at my eyes. I point them at the ground and start the long walk home.

I've thought before about all the times this has happened, trying to spot a pattern, to break the code. But the bubble doesn't know reason: all it knows is where to find you, and how to choke. Sometimes it comes slowly, from far away, like a storm cloud; other times it's fast and rough, like a clenching fist. When I can see it coming, I try and make sure I'm alone: no-one wants to see this, and even if anyone was willing to climb inside with me, there's no way there'd be enough room for two, not once it starts to get close. It's something you just can't get used to: looking out at familiar surroundings, feeling that creeping dread, fighting a muted battle with a screaming claustrophobia. And once the first bubble has lined your gullet, after that final, desperate, petrifying closing when you and the bubble become one being, it forms a lining, sitting tight under your skin and deep inside your mind and you're changed, and your nerves pang louder and your hands get thin and you keep wondering how such a strange and disturbing thing could ever happen to – *you*.

Have you ever stayed under water for so long that the shapes blacken your eyes and your heart thrashes against its cage and as you grab and paw at the water it slips past so heavy in the whipping weeds that your chest starts to burst and your subconscious takes over and you – take a breath?

Well, cold water doesn't feel cold once it's in your lungs. It burns.

Sometimes someone comes and looks inside, and I respond with a soap bubble and they act as though it was words and then they go away again. It seems strange, to me, that my way of living seems so normal to them. Sometimes I wish one of them would say, *What the fuck. Stop it. Speak words. Come out.* But they can see right through to my staring eyes, and to them a soap bubble seems just the same as a word.

Sometimes I think about the person I was when I was a child. That pocket-sized man with his bright eyes and soft, plump hands – and I wonder whether he and I are even the same person. He used to suffer, but he still used to smile; he used to look to the future as a grand, sparkling palace with more rooms than could ever be explored, and he used to peek through the thresholds and wonder what each one might be like. When he spoke, his words burst out clear and true, and he never grabbed his aching face or let out involuntary sighs or choked on hot bubbles in front of buses full of strangers. Am I the only person he could ever have become? Did God look down on him, mocking, seeing the whole road paved in front of him, the trap already set? Maybe that first encroaching bubble was something inevitable, maybe it was written in his make-up. Maybe that little child's insides were always lined with clingfilm, even before he knew it. Or maybe not. Maybe it was a product of all those things he saw and all the things that I've done.

Sometimes I see people and I think, *you've been trapped by a bubble too.*

And some of them have choked even harder than me; I can recognise the signs. That woman in tattered clothes who glides down the street, hunched over, crooning at her little straw doll; or the man who jabbers and spits in the London station, his eyes opaque like coloured marbles. Sometimes I look at someone like that and I remember that they were once a soft-handed child, just as I was. That they once looked out into their own palace, and thought, *I wonder what all these rooms have in store for me.* That God, or some other cruel person, must have held them down and forced suds into their throat. Sometimes, something strange comes over me, and I start to think that maybe I shouldn't avert my eyes, or clutch my bag close, or pretend not to have seen. That perhaps I have the chance to be the first one who's reached out and touched their shrink-wrapped skin – maybe that month, maybe even in years. I start to think that maybe, one day, I might extend a single human hand, reach in, grab their arm, and just say,

Stop.

Come out.

Are you OK?

THE OTHER SIDE OF THE ISLAND
Honor Levenson-Gower

In late autumn there is a big spring tide
We are crossing the strand to Vallay Island
Wet drained sands laced with green
Woven with ripples and rivulets

Spray from our glistening tyres
A consistent sleek wet sound
Ahead lies a green oasis
Topped off with a monolithic mansion
A crumbling edifice

The roof has succumbed
Stone pillars have lost their pinnacles
Rusty metal railings are bowed
The track is mud
We are surrounded by highland cows

Large shaggy heads and eyes
Belie what can be a grumpy disposition
Framed by majestic horns
Watching our progress

Following faint impressions of previous exploration
We reach the other side of the island
Green pasture fringes Atlantic shore
Grey granite is buried in the whitest beach
Azure waves flounce with white spume

Draining back over glistening sand
Out of the car we step down through the rocks
Stamp our signature across the empty bay
Imprint footsteps into the untouched emptiness
Clamber over a small headland of boulders
Another expanse of pure Hebridean shoreline shines ahead

THE OTHER SIDE OF THE ISLAND

And a mangle of ancient pots
Over the seas we make out the many islands of the sound
Far beyond the hills of Harris reach into the clouds
The sun is low at this time of year
It picks out the bright colours of flotsam
Alien on this isolated wilderness

We inspect each find discussing origin
On and on we walk until the end
The last dune climbed, we scrutinise the Uist Beach
There is someone walking dogs like us
Tiny distant figures

Turning back we keep to the Machair
Maran grass flowing, pointing the way
Tired legs carry us back
The wind in our faces dries our eyes
Finally, we spot the car

All loaded up the wheels slush along the tattoo of our arrival
Legs dangle from the tailgate
Back before the tide, it's turned

YOU'RE IMPOSSIBLE (CAN'T IMAGINE LIFE WITHOUT YOU)
Dana Liew Qi-e

A good casino never sleeps. The Elysian, however, could not be called a particularly good casino by any stretch of the imagination – when it sinks into a light doze in the small hours of the morning, he isn't particularly surprised. In the long hours just before dawn, the lights dim – the chatter winds down into a murmur. A janitor sidles down the aisle, mop in hand and eyes downcast. The patrons whisper low enough that the jangle of the slots machines turns jarring. There are no windows, but sometimes the door is thrown open and sunlight streams in, weak and warm and pale.

It is in this hushed moment that the bartender leans back onto the back-bar and lets out a long sigh. Most of the cocktail waitresses have retreated into the staff room, and the few patrons who want drinks will have to pay for them at the bar now that dawn has come. He wipes down a glass with clean quick strokes and slots it back onto the shelf with a flourish.

"Andy!" somebody calls. He scowls and turns.

Sarah is standing in front of him, dressed in what must be the most provocative dress to ever grace the floors of this casino. Eyelashes perfectly curled, heels near-impossibly high. Short blonde hair curling above her bare shoulders, a few locks resting on top of her generous cleavage.

Deliberately, he picks up another dirty glass from the bar. Then he turns his back on her. She's being ridiculous again, and he isn't having any of it.

"Oh come on," she moans, somehow making those words sound absolutely *filthy*. The heavy accent – he can't quite place where he's heard it from, but it's unmistakably foreign – certainly doesn't help. "*Andrew*, don't be like that."

He doesn't need to look to know what she's doing. Sarah's settling onto the creaky bar seat, leaning heavily onto the counter. She'd done that yesterday, and the day before yesterday, and the day the day before yesterday – and at this point he'd just about memorised her whole routine out of brute force repetition.

YOU'RE IMPOSSIBLE (CAN'T IMAGINE LIFE WITHOUT YOU)

"I came all this way to see you!" she complains, and the counter shifts ever so slightly. His frown deepens, but he still turns back to face her. The Boss would have his head if she caught him ignoring a paying customer, and he knew better than to hope that the woman wouldn't be willing to pay.

"You shouldn't be here," he says instead, sighing when the woman perks up at his acknowledgement. "Matt won't be happy with you when you get back home."

"Fuck Matt," she grins, snaps her fingers. He rolls his eyes and starts preparing the usual. "Didn't come to America to stay home and play housewife."

He slides the little pink umbrella into the glass. Her smile only widens. Insufferable as always. He tells himself that the only reason why his chest feels warm is because of faulty air-conditioning. He slept late last night. The air is full of dust. He should really tell someone about that.

"Why do you keep coming here?" he despairs, and swipes another dirty glass from the counter so he can at least pretend he's still working. "I overcharge you for every drink you buy."

The woman just winks at him and downs it in a single gulp.

"That's thirty dollars, by the way."

"Only thirty." she purrs, produces the money from the gap between her cleavage and slides it across the table. Why does she insist on doing this? He uses the bottom of the cleaned glass to scoot the money behind the counter so he can pick it up later, his frown turning almost petulant when the woman laughs at him.

"You must be warming up to me," she smiles, low and dirty. Not deterred in the slightest. "Was fifty yesterday."

"It'll be fifty again if you don't stop doing that," he threatens, rolling his eyes when the positively insufferable woman just presses her perfectly manicured hand to her perfectly scarlet lips, holding back a giggle.

He bites back a groan. If any other person tried this kind of nonsense on him he would have long since kicked them out. Sarah, however, has a gift for making ridiculously over-the-top flirting, charming. Somehow. It's all in the intent – he's reasonably sure she doesn't actually expect anything out of this. A few weeks ago he'd told her he was ace, and she'd responded by doing positively obscene things to the pink umbrella in her drink.

That was awkward to explain to the Boss.

He slides a new drink over to her. Years of practice dealing with patrons allow him to keep a straight face when she fingers the tip of the umbrella in it, ever so slightly. It really doesn't help that she's still smiling.

"You wouldn't," she states confidently, taking a long sip and sighing at the taste. "Exquisite as always, darling."

"I would," he says conversationally, cognizant of any outside attention. There aren't any patrons near the bar now, good- and the Boss isn't nearby, either. He takes her glass to start mixing her a new drink. "Everything alright at home? How're the kids?"

A beat of silence, and Sarah gives up all pretence of dignity and flops face first onto the countertop. He scoops the drink out of her hand before she can spill it all over herself.

"He hates me!" she wails, then flops her arms around like a dying fish. One of the part-time janitors shoots her a dirty look, and he responds by glaring right back at the offending bastard. They turn away quickly. Good.

"Your son doesn't hate you," he soothes, because this is the third time she'd come in to complain about the little gremlin this week and he can garner a guess to as to who "he" is. "He's five. He probably doesn't even know what the word means."

"He does," she insists, mumbling into the grain of the sticky countertop. "He does, and he's using it all the time, and he hates me." She looks up. Her make-up isn't smudged at all, which he attributes to witchcraft. "Andrew, what am I gonna do?"

"Buy him a sword," he deadpans. The first few times he'd offered her actual solutions, but she clearly just wanted a listening ear. Why not get some fun out of it?

"Boys love swords," he asserts, hands her back her drink. "The bigger, the sharper and the heavier, the better."

Sarah perks up, a glint of mischief in her eye. "That's a *brilliant* idea."

Oh god, no. "Sarah," he says slowly. "No."

"Sarah, yes," she replies, then whips out her phone. The smile that crosses her face, then, is the smile of a woman who has found benediction. "You're a goddamn genius, that's what you are. I'm going to buy him the biggest damn sword on the bloody Internet."

"Is that even legal?"

"No harm in trying," she practically chirps.

He can't help but laugh, then, fondness curling the edges of his lips up. Happiness tucked tight in his heart. She's impossible, she really is. "Just try it, Sarah. Just try it."

BANGKOK INCENSE HOLDERS
Charles Lobo-Clarke

They bear tacky
tropical tattoos:

stars up the spine,
Om sign on the sternum.

Mine's worn-down;
scorch-scarred

from holidays of
smoky sensuality.

You can buy them cheap
in oriental markets,

standing on the corner
right next to the fake jewellery,

marble elephants,
Pikachu puppets,

two-quid buddhas,
synthetic harem pants,

yin-yang keychains,
and Same Same

But Different
T-shirts

in English
and in Asianese.

GROWN UP
Chris Matthews

They had tried to scrub them out. But the markings remained on the utility room wall. Each marking was similar: a scrawled star, a line, and another star. Then numbers. All the lines were neatly stacked up. They reminded her of the rope captains used in the olden days to measure speed – with knots. A knot, a line, and another knot. Here, the highest line isn't that high at all. It's three eleven. But she hadn't seen it in a while. Hasn't been back. Hasn't gone down the hall past the washing machine, drying rack, and vacuum cupboard. She remembers him as he was. So wonderful, wasn't it? Smile, kid, stand straight, yep, three twelve – wait, wait, no tippy toes mind. So? So, eleven. Leven? That's it. Can I play football now? Go for it then. Yeah? Yes, be back before six. And then peace. Peace. Need this. Needed it. The quiet, silence. Before the turn around hands on table, turn around say again. The wait, wait, no. If she could've torn down the numbers on the wall. Could've collected them. Added them up to six foot six: that would be fine. But markings don't move. Markings don't hide. Even if they do manage to paint – to smear them over – the thin lines will remain as shadows.

[NOUN]
Lucy May

I run *beautiful* over my tongue, around my

mouth behind my lips, it sprints so I

run, tuck the *beautiful* under my tongue but

licks of anger   split

           spitting   teeth bared   bare stripped into b

    eau ti ful you can't bear

the nines   strip me off rip my clothes tip *beautiful* into a song along

that curved line of b

        ody. The beautiful

    doesn't quite.

    It doesn't require a [   ]. It does not and it is   not.

Rage comes in

    my & you & I & we & us

naked formless B & E, A U & T, I F, U & L. Supplementary.

The *beautiful* is not "beautiful" because it depends upon a [   ].

So when the [   ] is a mere hole, what will

be   come of us

beach comb ers hunting for treasure like children for stones

for   *golden* as hot liquid lovers melting the language of man

      bending mouths out of shape spines in the wake of *precious*

                preciously precocious we take caution

[NOUN]

                                              blows us away

                                     wings wind and wind exhales like

words. So much of it mapped upon the [   ], dependent upon the touch

If   the sound

is the word, and the

word gives a whole, and the whole

is fleshed with adjectives then I want to cup the *blue*

pretty is cooling in the palm of my hand, I've

picked *darling* out from a seabed and counted its legs

            like a crab encrusted by corals. Beautiful

      oceans, solid salt below where all of

my claws are grabbing

B & *E* is lost to where

           the *A U T* caved, clunking as *I* sunk

                &   drowned   among   *F*   *U*   *L*

   a seabed wreathed in nouns.

THE TRAGEDY OF THE MAN ON THE MOON
Magdalena Meza-Mitcher

When I was still small enough
to be held when I cried,
my mother would sing to me
a story about the boy
who spent his life asleep
in the craters of the moon
and his days in between
everything else.

Never leaving,
he dreamed of shining lights,
laughing stars in his dark universe.
He imagined flying between worlds;
running faster until
he taunted with each step
a rainbow stream behind.

Music filled his dreams -
a peculiar sound to him.
Notes danced in his mind
scaling the highest mountains
he could paint, then falling
to the craters.
Trying to sing along,
he found his voice sleeping still.

Once, the boy opened his eyes
for a shooting star moment,
and he found the dust around him
damp, his cheeks weeping,
so he never opened them again.

THE TRAGEDY OF THE MAN ON THE MOON

The sight of his sadness
woke up his voice,
but it simply could not sing.
If he only stopped staring
at the ground around him
and, for once, looked up
he would see the lights of his dreams
flying above his head
and the music he longed for waiting
among the laughter of the stars.

This, my mother would hum to me.
We still wait for a voice to sing back.

COURT
Magdalena Meza-Mitcher

Remember the room:
bookcases stuffed with old spines,
air dusty with words.
Two sworn testimonies, one
gift-wrapped restraining order.
"For what it's worth,"
hair slicked with slimy defence,
"we all believed you."
Ushered out, underhand deal,
hushed voices conspire, "That's her."

PILLOW TALK
Magdalena Meza-Mitcher

Cotton on skin, warmer than him.
Steady breathing lifts the duvet up,
before it floats down. Feather filled dreams
take flight above our heads.
Can't they see us?
Can his fingertips reach my lower back
and trace a gentle apology
across the no man's land between us?
Asleep, he's just as distant to me
as in the light of morning.
Should I be mourning the fire
that lived in him, that sailed out
to the crematorium -a single row boat-
before he burnt out?
These suffering words travel in single file
across my pillow to his;
lonely pilgrimage.
Can his soul reach me from there
or did it get lost on the way?
Do the lines etched into your palm
remember my kisses
as the rings in a cut down tree
remember the wind's caresses?

DRIVE
Millie Norman

Joanne's standing on the driveway she left her mother screaming on five years before. Remembers how the sobs went silent when she slammed the car door. How she watched her sink out of the frame of her rear-view mirror like a beheading. Black night. Amber lights on and steaming out into the rain. Thought her stomach would settle when she pulled away but felt it strapped to the wheel, turning and turning and crushed into the gravel. Radio *ch-ch-changes* cut silent with the blink of a call *tuuuurn and face the strange* and a call *and these children that yooou spit on as they tryyy and change their* and a call *time may change me but you can't trace*. And a call. How she rolled the window down threw her phone out onto the concrete lit a fag shouted FUCK over the hum of the news roundup felt the tears and the snot begin to fuse and then roll and then seep and then land like a flood on her lips. Drove until she stopped being able to see.

Joanne feels the tears begin to roll now and tries to suck them back up. Feels Mark's small hand light on her back like he's afraid she'd snap in two if he presses down.

I know you miss her. Fingertips graze shoulder blades. *Lieke—your mum— she wouldn't have minded. About. You know.* Swallows. *She would have been so happy to have you here, Jo.*

Snorts *Fuck off Mark, you don't know shit* and strides into the house gnawing her cheek to stop the shakes. Tastes copper in her mouth.

*

She didn't go to the funeral last week. Sat curled in her bed with her phone next to her face in the black, only half-reading when it lit to remind her to **Check-In and Print the Boarding Pass**. Amber leaking into the room through the curtain when it told her to **Make Way to the Gate**. Felt her body dissolve. Swallowed by the mattress. Slept through the daylight and into the dark only half-noticing when her phone lit with the blink of a text.

R u out of passport control yet? Waiting by drop-off but think will get moved on soon. Mark x

And a call.

Parked at short stay will come in to find u. Do u want coffee? Mark x

And a call.

Jo????

Looked at her body and tried to call it her name. Jo???? Limbs there. Brain somewhere else.

And a call.

It's your mum's funeral, Jo. Pls call me.

Imagined him on the other end of the phone line. In a cheap suit. Cheap flowers. Sat on a cheap wooden pew surrounded by people Lieke barely knew. Watching them perform their grief. Choruses of *Nothing To Be Done. If Only She'd Asked For Help* like she hadn't been howling for it all her fucking life. Wiping their misrouted tears. Looking at him like he was a three-legged dog. Sucked into hugs meant to shift the guilt from their bodies to his. *She Really Seemed To Get Better When You Two Got Together Mark. But Nothing That Could Be Done.* Like fuck. Outside the crematorium, watching the smoke run ribbons.

Unscrewed a bottle of wine and swigged. Tears rolled seeped landed like a flood on her lips. Hers? Felt the pillow wet. Swigged. Guilt like flames in her belly. Curled in a ring on the bed. Made sounds she didn't recognise. Cut silent with the blink of a call.

Oh my god Jo, thank fuck.

I'm s-sosorry Mark I'm so—so

I understand, it's okay. Are you okay? Are you with someone?

HA…HA! You're such a fucking wet wipe Mark.

Beat.

Have you been drinking?

What…f-fuck…fuck up. Fuck do you--fuck do you care.

Beat.

Of course I fucking care, Jo.

Beat.

I'm s-sorry. I didn't mean that.

Beat.

Will you come and stay with me for a few days? I want—I think it would be good for you to come back. You know. Help with the—

Yeah. Yeah I'll come. S-sorry.

Click.

*

The kettle clicks. Sighs to fill the silence left as the hiss of the steam fades out. Back turned. Pouring.

You don't take sugar, do you Jo?

Oh, no, that's fine as it is. Cheers.

Silence. Only the echoes of the room. Bass burrowing deep into her skull. Tries not to remember.

How was your journey?

Oh. Long, you know.

Bass tunnelling into the depths of her ear canals. Memories like tinnitus. Counters the dull hum with

How's work?

Oh. I've been on leave for a few months.

Beat.

Back on Monday. I'm thinking about retraining, though. Teaching, maybe. Or going travelling. Something.

Off to find yourself? Smirks.

Bit rich from you.

They laugh with a weight.

Still with that lad?
Snorts. *What, Adam? Fuck off.*

That was it, Ponytail fucking Adam. Christ. You were besotted with him.

Oh come off it—

Nah, you were! Remember when me and Li came to visit? The look on your mum's face when he brought out that fucking, oh, what was it?

Falafel and it was—

Oh, FALAFEL! Fuckin—

--and it was fucking nice!

Fucking cardboard!

Yeah, mum told him that and all! He cried all bloody evening.

Belly laughs. Sighs as the silence sets in.

That can't have been the last time I saw you, Jo.

Beat.

Yeah, no it was. Tinnitus. Burrowing in the. Tries not to remember but she. *She was still sober then.*

Beat.

Yeah. That's right. She was.

Beat.

Well. I've missed having you about, love.

Beat.

*

Flames in her belly. Tries not to remember a childhood spent looking through keyholes and being scared of things-that-go-bump-in-the-night. Hide and seek. Tries not to remember adult whisperings and raucous smokers' laughter rippling in toyshop eardrums. Keys grinding in locks. *Go to bed.* Nursing crimson nosebleeds. Tries not to remember but sees the dark red stains on the dark wooden table where she ate Coco-Pops and drank apple juice on birthdays. Smoothing foundation over bruises. Tries not to remember holding her mother's hair back while she vomited into the last bright thrusts of the morning (*you had to leave*) but can still feel the greasy strands. Shower head over the bath tub. *I'm so* gag *I'm so sorry* lurch *I'm so sorry Joanne* and sobs in shakes Joanne was too young to understand. Hoovering up glass. *You're so good.*

Tries not to remember being held by her mother on the map of her lap but can remember the exact contour lines she was pinned to on those days she felt so certain they could travel through all the muddy lakes and marshland as-the-crow-flies. Tries not to remember how she tried to tell Joanne about art on those brighter mornings where she'd sit outside and smoked and drank coffee. Tries not to remember her favourite artist was a French Modernist who loved troubled women and tries not to remember how her mother loved men who loved troubled women. Baccy crumbs next to breadcrumbs. *It's just you and me, Jo.*

Tries not to remember YOU ARE THE ONLY ONE I (plates colliding with the kitchen wall like meteorites) tries not to remember YOU'RE THE BEST THING THAT EVER (cigarettes pressed into stomach and elbows and once her forehead for one two three) tries not to remember PLEASE DON'T FUCKING. LEAVE. Swimming in her eardrum as she drove away.

Brain there. Limbs somewhere else.

Where are you going, Jo?

I'm just going out for a bit. For a drive. Tries to recognise her voice. Untangle the sounds.

You've driven eight hours today, love. Just take a--

I'll be back soon. I promise.

Out of the yellow and into the black.

*

Joanne sits in her car and necks the rum until she feels her insides glowing, pulsing gold. Flames in her belly. Vision mellowed like a washed-out glaucoma. Soft jaw. Takes another shot and winces but leaves the bottle top off. Kicks legs up onto the dashboard and watches them slip down. Snorts. Kicks legs back up and rolls a cigarette. Lights it. Flames in her belly. Eyes roll back slowly in her sockets. Calm ecstasy. Snaps body back up and punches the dial of the radio *by the time I thought I'd got it maaade it seemed the taste was not so sweet.* Black night. Amber lights on and steaming out into the rain *how the ooothers must see the faaaker I'm much too fast to take that test ch-ch-ch.* Watches the smoke run ribbons round her fingers and presses the amber tip into her thigh for one two three. *Ch-ch-chang-es.* Snorts. Punches the dial. Throws the cigarette out of the window onto the concrete shouts FUCK and with that she's out of the car and into the night.

She's in the club. Shot. Feels her body dissolving. Pulsing sweating shaking under the neon. Strobes making her body a flip-book. This stop-motion woman. Shot. Bass burrowing deep. Paints spheres with her arms around her head. Moves in great, deliberate lines. Eyes rolled back in their sockets. She's a magic trick. Lids shut. Shot. Flames in her belly. Molten veins. Feels her body dissolve. Pale meat *(you had to leave)* and puzzle bones. Limbs loose around the room. Shot. Fingers chained to the man with the buzzcut's neck. Lips clamped to his earlobe. Hips bound between the walls of his hands. Stomach strapped to the. Watches herself evaporate.

Feels his breath hot on her neck. Keys grinding in locks. Bass rippling in her eardrums. Neon lights on and steaming out into the sweat. Feels her body dissolve *(you had to leave)*. And the stomach. The stomach. Feels his hands in her greasy hair *(you had to leave)*. Flames in her. Tries not to but she. Hands crushing her contour lines. Lids shut. Hide and seek *(you had to leave)*. Breath hot on her neck. Bass grinding in her eardrums. Neon steam. Feels her body. The stomach. Pale meat *(you had to leave)*. Greasy hair. Flames. Crushing into the gravel. Tries not to but she. *You're trouble, babe.* Breath hot in her eardrums. Neon flames. Grinding locks. The stomach. Crushed into the. Tries not to but she. The dial. Molten veins. The stomach. Tries not to but she. Punches the *WHAT THE FUCK YOU BITCH?*

Leaves him screaming. Runs. Into the. Rain. Had to. Slams car door. Black. Amber. Stomach strapped to the. Shot. Flames in her. Had to. Gravel. Blink of a. Vision like. Gone like a. Beheading. Shot. Lights fag. Twists end into the stomach for one two three. Face wet from tears. Flood. Snot. Hers? Shot. Blink of a. Cut silent. *I watch the ripples change their siiiiize but never leave the stream.* Keys grinding in the ignition. Hum. Has to leave. Lands on her lips like a. Drove until she

REMAINS
Amber Otton-Miller

You button up your lips and stuff them inside of your mouth because this body is now clothing, now casing, now shell.
Two hearts beat in the same rhythm, same body,
                                            but not the same body
just the same casing, same shell, tucked up snugly inside each other like Matryoksha dolls.

Phone call, he rips the
buttons off your lips. He's 147 miles away yet the words
bubble up and boil over, you can feel them dissecting him into
indistinguishable slivers of sentences served up as he tries to make sense of it.
                                              By 'it' you mean her.
There is only evidence of her in the positive cross (that's more of a negative), and in
black and white images he never had to see, never
got to see her sucking her thumb. He only has
memories of her from you, and those are not memories of her but feelings,
memories of feelings.
memories of feelings.
When it's time, you tremble like your bones are tectonic plates colliding. The machine stutters and latches onto you,
                 and you let it
                        tear the
                                    fruit from the stem
                                                    until all that's left is
                               blackcurrant jam dribbling out of you and
you lay her to rest in this crevice of void inside of you that is not empty itself
                                                              but empty of life.
                                        Your clothes fit you again, but your
                         body does not. It feels like crawling into bed when
your lover is missing, you have all this   space and their imprint is all that
                                                                               remains.

REMAINS

Eventually no evidence remains but
memory on the cusp of every conscious thought, and it
lingers, not like the kiss of an old lover but like an old
broken bone that still aches in the cold -
still weak.

THE END
Cara Ow

It is Wednesday and I am sitting at the desk watching myself grow into the furniture. There's nothing much you can do anymore, now that the apocalypse has been declared. The snow's toxic and the air will kill you, plus the TV only blares out old Trump interviews after Elon Musk took all our celebrities to Mars.

It wasn't always like that. I actually had a part-time job at Auntie Anne's, believe it or not, but Mr Lang had to let go of me in August because "screaming at kids about the end of the world isn't exactly in line with our company policy, Sarah." Dad says some people can't handle the truth. I say I know. Mum says my god the both of you are crazy please hand over the phone Kenny Tan that's quite enough from you.

That was the last time I spoke to them. I didn't even say "Goodbye" like it was final—I said "zài jiàn" in Chinese, which is stupid of me because it doesn't actually mean "bye I'm off to die now this is it thanks for being Mum and Dad". It means "see you again" as if there was ever the hope of buying more time in Mandarin. That's the trouble—Chinese people always think that we can bargain our way through life, even in end-of-the-world type of situations. If it's unfair, we'd shout our way to God or whoever the hell's up there watching us die, and demand for more hours to do what's necessary before…you know. I try not to think it over, because then my head will spill with too much, but now that we're on it maybe if I had more time I'd fly home and hug my dad, kiss my cat, pop my cherry, take a chance! Talk to Jules, do something bizarre – I don't know – invent a time machine so that Peter Yates didn't have to go all those months back. But of course, that's just me again, trying to plug the endless *what if*s with more and more crazy-talk.

Yates was our lecturer that term and we were moving on to *The Prelude* when it all began. I was uncharacteristically awake in the LT because a) Jules was in the seat behind and b) Peter Yates was turning blue in the face. I thought that it was one of those ageing things, one of those Fogey Old Men Things, but after forty minutes it seemed to me that all this coughing was becoming excessive.

"Now let's analyse," –cough– "Wordsworth's fixation," –cough– cough– "on rustic" –cough– "living. How great it is to be" –cough–cough– cough– "alive and yo–" – final cough – thud.

And then all hell broke loose.

THE END

Well, people *said* that it was chaos. Apparently a lot of them were screaming, but in my head there was only silence. I remember sitting there—it must have looked strange—just staring and staring at Yates' white hands like water biscuits all pockmarked with age. It's a funny thought, but I think hands are the most private parts of our anatomy. Ever notice how people sit on their palms during interviews? It's a way of saying, *shut up don't tell the boss I'm faking my credentials!* Hands tell their own story separate from the main body. It deviates from the narrative, but sometimes, the things they speak of tell you more than what you were looking for.

I fell in love with Jules' hands first. Everything else, the hair, the nose, even the eyes, came crashing after. It's ridiculous—I'm speaking of this as if falling in love means plummeting down a dark hole with him at the end, his arms outstretched, palms turned upwards. But if that were so, I spotted Jules' hands first before knowing it was safe to land. It must have been in class when it happened. He was picked to read his poetry, and I was a bit miffed at having been glanced over. Back then, everything about him screamed blasé—the way he sat, slouched into his seat, then that voice, how it slurred together, and would you look at those shoes? He obviously cared about nothing at all, and I would have gone on thinking that way about him until I saw his hands that told me otherwise. They were surprising to see, fingers all spidery and tall, coloured like tea, over-steeped; in their softness I thought they belonged to a girl. See, the boys back home have swollen scabs for fingers—they leave dark marks on your skin that sink so deep, even six hours with the shower on doesn't scrub anything off. No one tells you how love should feel, but looking at Jules' hands, the way they curled around that sheet of paper all soaked through with worry; how light that touch must be; those palms in a cradle as if handling some small animal… And there I was, thinking it must be love if it's all bruises and pruned skin when here you have Jules and his hands that make you hopeful for something kind and quite tender—from someone with holes in his Nikes, no less.

On the day of Yates' death, I was staring at his hands wondering what they would tell me, like a surprise-I'm-still-alive kind of wiggle maybe, or some sort of Jules-esque revelation, when – "WHATTHEHELLAREYOUDO-INGCOMEONLET'SGETOUTOFHERE!" I don't really remember what happened after that, or even how we left it, but I guess you can say that's how Jules and I properly met. With him yelling in my ear.

In case you were hoping for anything, I'd say: quash that thought. It's the apocalypse. All hope ends here—the girl never gets to see the boy again. After that lecture, all our classes got cancelled. I guess the university doesn't like the idea of anyone dying publicly, even if they know that everyone is suffering. They'd rather us do it privately, in our own times, in our own rooms. It's something I try not to puzzle out too much, because it's probably another British thing that I won't get—this idea of being "anti-social". Our Vice-Chancellor addressed that in an email, the one telling us of a) The Biological Apocalypse and b) how Yates died from air poisoning. Our VC said that it was bad manners of Yates to go off in that way, without any warning whatsoever, and yes, so what if it's The End, could you all just please die with a little more discretion?

So I'm at my desk trying to die nicely, but it's been a long while and my body's still not letting up. I don't want to move because people say you shouldn't die with any regrets, so sitting still's my way of not accumulating any more. But my brain's in backwash and I'm thinking of Yates – his hands – it's too much and I think I'm going to burst so I bolt out of my room and into the bar where all the kids are gathered to breathe in the smell of stale VKs stirred into the toxic air burning down our throats and I don't know who or what I'm looking for in this crowd but when I find Jules at the bay windows everything rests in a final full stop.

"You!" I shout. His head jerks up.

Already I feel the walls of my throat seaming together because that's probably not the way you should approach the Love of Your Life and I want to stop but I can't, not with him looking all open-faced and vulnerable grasping that glass to his chest so I'm squelching through the alcohol-soaked floor to him to say, "I don't know what I'm doing, but I'm saying this not because I'm hoping for anything – I mean, what can you possibly hope for now that it's The End – I *have* to – God, I'm sounding like a crazy person, but you'd be lying if you said you've never – I mean, if I don't say it now I'll just…die, right?"

And in that moment I thought of Mum and Dad, how I never got the Final Word, how Yates never got the Final Word, and maybe we're all just scared of having anything but the Right Words—well there's no such thing as the right phrasing only the present perfect and that's as good as it gets so even though I'm full of false starts and half-stops I can't go on missing the moment wishing for better when we only have the now, no matter how red-faced sweaty-palmed dry-mouthed it is because it is here and he is here and I am here and well what are you waiting for except your own death so –

"Jules Park," I say, "I fell in love with your hands."

Then I sit back, spent, because I've done it. I don't care anymore, don't need a response anymore, and so what if he's confused because what matters is that I've done it. Even if there was no hope wishing for dark alleyway kisses. And quiet cinema cuddles. Or footsie under the family table. Or waking up the next day with him in bed. Hair dream-tousled. The cat in the corridor crying for more milk. The laundry going on and on with all our coloured clothes and past lives tumbling into one another—no, none of that anymore. So I just stare at him and his hands as I've always done, and I guess he gets it because we sit there for a long time looking at each other. And maybe if we were in a different time and a different place without the world blowing itself up from behind the glass against our backs, then maybe someone far away would look at the both of us and see two kids falling in love or maybe even out of it as we sit stuck there in silence with nothing of the past or present or future hanging between our static heads.

THE STAIRCASE
Amy Pattison

It hangs itself in the woodland
By a desert clearing
Every traveller dissolves in the sunlight
Washed away by the wind

But not always
It doesn't happen always

Sometimes the creatures cry out
From behind their biblical texts
Reading reading always
Reading

But it doesn't read
It hangs itself in the woodland
A scab in the desert
A wounded staircase
Moulding, wilting
No blood left inside
The trees have wounded it
Rotting with November
The staircase is a spine
Twisted with scoliosis
It couldn't be there
It couldn't be, but it was

It's holding up the moon
Or maybe the moon is already up there
And the staircase is its veins
Hanging down
From the black universe

A traveller vomits by a tree

He remembers a city he went to once
Takes a step
Don't move too much or it will crumble to ashes

                                                                         What reality was it from?

With every step
A light turns on

                                                                         Will it eat him whole?

It hasn't got any teeth yet

With every step they get nearer to freedom
They think about the people who have ignored them
Crying again
Crying again
Their footsteps are muffled

                                                                    They might burst into flames

No, they can't
Oh, you're right, maybe they will

The moon twitches
And becomes the sun
Only the traveller's shoes are left behind
Burnt into the ground
Like in that city
That city far away
The traveller went there
He didn't understand their words
He burnt all of his postcards

Oh, no he didn't
That was in another city
Now he is just a shadow

The Staircase
Crumbles into white ashes

MARLBORO
Flo Pearce-Higginson

My god, he's gotten thin. Ugly, ill-looking, gaunt. His waistcoat sags around his pathetic, skeletal frame. He doesn't eat any more, he just smokes. That foul stench, I fucking hate it. It's everywhere in this squalid shithole of a room. The trains rattle outside. I envy them. Every hour they escape this place and move on to pastures new.

Oh shut up, I say to myself. If you're getting jealous of a metal box on wheels, you need a hobby. I raise myself from the chair, and slowly, clumsily, I lumber across the room. My book lies on the bedside table, my hardback friend. I've read it, eleven, twelve times now? The words blur together, the story monotonous, but anything beats a conversation with him. Dark, poisonous words, spat in my direction. The type to burn the ears upon hearing.

In the back of my mind, hovering out of my reach like a heatwave over burning asphalt, I remember a time when my feelings towards him were tender, when they were the things of freshly picked wildflowers, the sweet smoke of a bonfire, and the icy beauty of a November evening. I remember his iron grip. A time when his pig-headed stubbornness seemed like a determination, a defiance against the world, something to be admired. When his fingertips against my skin didn't send a fearful chill down my spine and bile to my mouth. All I feel for him now is seething, all-consuming rage which burns in my guts and makes me nearly blind with fury.

1986. That's when I first laid eyes on him. A forsaken day; and ironically, the most beautiful day I can remember. I had just started my nursing placement, and, fragile after a shift of dealing with a particularly tiresome patient, I arrived at my friend's party, and headed straight for the bar.

A whiskey on the rocks.

A mojito.

A cider. And then,

A curl of smoke. A whisper of him. Of my future being blasted to rack and ruin. Oh, that sweet smell. A sting in the nostrils. It seemed a sweet relief, even before he stepped into view. I was struck first by his voice: sharp as flint, a blade to slice your thumb upon. Through the smog, the stupor of my banal, stupid life, he appeared as a figure in the mist, a danger, or a saviour. Now I think of it, he has played both roles. He has brought me stability, a place to live, and all the material possessions I need. And in many ways, I should be grateful. I have much to thank him for. But every day, every hour, every minute, even, the thought of being free, of roaming the streets with nowhere to go, no one checking on me, no one following me, and no one caring about me, chases itself around my head like a dog mad with rabies. A beautiful image appears; all the years of tension that have built up inside me, twisting my guts and pressing my chest, burst from me in a scream of such strength and vigour that all these four wretched walls disintegrate into wailing dust and he chokes. Chokes on the years of my growing resentment, frustration, hatred.

The journey, from when that bloody cigarette smoke of his first invaded my nose, to where I sit now, my legs slowly sticking to this black, weathered leather chair, has been twisted, arduous, and degrading. Oh, so degrading. I am nothing now. The first few months, years, even, I was a dog basking in the sun; content, warm and loved. However, as the years went on, I came to understand that I was really a deer in headlights. Almost waiting to be maimed. The real question, though, is whether it is the fault of the deer, running into the road so recklessly, or the fault of the driver, for not being cautious? Or even the fault of the road, which shouldn't be crossing the deer's habitat in the first place? Is it my fault, for allowing myself to be so captivated by him that I willingly walked into his web? His fault, for being such a heartless bastard that he neither knows nor cares that I sit here, boiling with rage and age old fear, because of him? Or even fate's fault, for making me agree to go to that wretched party, for staying near the bar? For not making me run for the hills when that sting scorched my nostrils?

You make yourself stupid with these questions.

Shut up.

What has happened, has happened. You can muse about why a cat kills a mouse for fun for years, but you stand to only waste your time and your mind. It is a fact of life. Move on.

My mind drifts for a few moments, hounding the departing train down the scuffed steel tracks. Who knows where we will go. Maybe somewhere by a lake. Yes. Cool, calm, clear water, occasionally disturbed by gusts of wind. A willow, tendrils grasping for the surface of the water, snatching at the air. Distant cries of geese, swooping overhead in formation. I am safe. By my lake I am safe.

He coughs. I jerk, fleeing my lake. He doesn't even turn his head; he never does these days. Instead his cough fades to vapour, misting the thin glass in front of him. I watch his cheekbones sink in and out discordantly as he puffs away. Inhale, exhale. I gaze at him, with a sort of twisted amusement. Sometimes, a piece of my old self appears, and whines; oh, what has he done to make you hate him so? And in all honesty, I really don't know. It's as if he's done nothing to earn my hatred, but also that he's worked for years to make me hate him. I'm confused in my own mind as to why I've drifted so far from him, after initially clinging on for dear life. The obvious answers seem to be his total lack of interest, and his cold hearted tendency to destroy and decimate anything I seem even close to enjoying. And yet; perhaps I should have been kinder. He has suffered greatly in the past: losing a father and a brother to the war before he was ten years old. I get the sense that he walks around with walls up. All emotions must show their papers before entrance, and many get turned away. There is no stronger security anywhere.

I should have tried harder. The window faded years ago, the time in which I could have helped him. There was a time, when he collapsed the walls sometimes. Let me in. But even then, I didn't want to help him. I had grown fearful of him, and was terrified of what I would find behind the wall.

No! Why should I have done more? Why should I be obligated to help someone who refuses to be helped? He has treated me like a frustrating piece of dirt that refuses to come off the bottom of his shoe for years. Never once have I felt appreciated, understood, or tolerated. There is only so much indifference a person can take, only so much cruelty. He claims that I am lucky to keep my hardback friend, that it won't be taken away like all the others. He doesn't even enjoy the power: to him it seems obvious that he must keep me beneath his thumb. It is a fact of life. So many times, I have thought that I have reached the edge, that I will not take anymore. Never has this got further than a thought, however. Perhaps today is different. I shift in my seat. Another train rattles by. Another escapee.

I grasp my hardback friend, digging my fingers into the cracked leather cover. I stare at him. His eyes, chips of dirty ice hammered into his sunken sockets, gaze lazily out at the station, completely uninterested. Those eyes of his pierce right through me, make me a child cowering under another blow. For all my boiling hatred, one flicker of movement from him and all that is real to me is metallic fear in my mouth. The day outside is beautiful, but it does nothing for me.

In the sunlight that streams through the window, the dust motes swirl, dancing a jig far beyond my understanding. But then; an intruder. A single grey hair, bleached white by the sun, drifts down into my solace, disturbing the dust.

I feel a hot acidic rage build in my chest. Is nothing sacred, can nothing just be mine anymore? I want to slam my hardback friend shut and beat him round the head with it.

I'm going to do it.

I'm going to escape.

Silently, I close the book, the pages merging once more. I clutch it, my hand slippery with sweat. I raise it, ready to strike, a coiled snake.

He flicks his burnt out cigarette out of the window. I freeze.

"Go get me a pack of smokes, will you?" he mutters, not even turning to me. In dead silence, I rise, and leave him, slamming the door behind me.

HOW MUCH IS A LIFE WORTH?
Chiara Picchi

Thunder booms. Lightning strikes. Rain whips concrete and flesh alike, made sharp by the wind; layers of clouds have choked the sun, turning day into night and heat into frigidness. The streets are deserted, left to the fury of the elements as they stare at the single shadow braving the weather.

The cold seeps through Azrael's jacket and closes its claws around his bones, turning them brittle as his clothes weigh down on him, made heavy by too many hours spent under the deluge. His teeth chatter and hands shake, buried deep into his pockets. He wishes he hadn't lost his phone- he knows the way to Mr. Mercer's shop but the rain creates a blurred barrier in his vision, it is difficult to know if he is on the right path.

Goddamn British climate. He avoids a puddle, makes a turn into a side alley. A moan echoes off the stone, so feeble Azrael almost misses it amidst the howling of the wind. He trips over a foot before he sees the figure folded on the ground. Winter is a dreadful season to be homeless – the old man's lips are blue, his limbs stiff, frozen solid, but there is still a sliver of life clinging to the body. Azrael kneels down. A mouth moves to form a cry for help – he ignores it. He must be quick, there isn't much time left. He slides his bag off his aching shoulders and extracts a vial.

The shivering ceases, the pleas fall silent, eyes glaze over and a stream of opaque liquid slithers down the corner of the man's mouth. He is quick to bottle it. One has to be careful, it doesn't take much for it to evaporate- God knows how many lives and souls have been lost forever that way. The vial joins its comrades in Azrael's bag- he hopes there are enough.

Perhaps he will be lucky and come across another stray cat: they are big enough to make a consistent loot without raising suspicion. He moves quickly – closing time is nearing and he needs to reach the shop before it is too late: he hasn't done all this work for nothing.

The insignia is faded, washed away by decades of rain. He pushes the door open - a bell chimes his arrival, a cobweb oscillates.

The air is stale and laced with dust – the latter floats in the air and clings to the window panes, obfuscating them, blocking any look at the outside world. Textiles crowd the shop, crawling with fleas that Azrael hopes will prefer the warmth of their nests to his soaked clothing.

The place looks abandoned, perhaps he received the wrong information. Maybe he took a wrong turn or confused roads, surely this cannot be it. Water drips from his jacket onto the floorboards and melds with the grime coating them, seeping into the wood to form maroon stains. His nose itches, irritated by the stench of mould and damp. Maybe he is wasting his time. Maybe he should go back home, before his mother finds out he was here in the first place.

The floorboards cave in and creak as a hand pokes through pieces of fabric hanging from the ceiling to reveal a mane of hair. The young man's heart jumps into his throat.

"What are you doing here kid?"

Mr. Mercer's voice resonates across the shop, so deep that Azrael can feel it vibrating in his chest. His presence towers in the room- he seems too large for it; it's a miracle he can fit at all.

"You have something I need."

"If you're looking for textiles you're in the wrong place. I've been out of business for years."

"It's not cloth I'm after."

The man's clear eyes fixate on him and Azrael can see his brain working behind them, its mechanisms spinning in an attempt to decipher the visitor. He scratches his beard - if its length and unruliness are any indication, it hasn't seen a razor in quite some time. The young man wouldn't be surprised if it were infested with fleas as well.

"How old are you?"

"Twenty-four."

Laughter booms, exposing the plethora of stains and putrefaction that coat Mercer's teeth.

"Don't lie boy, that beard of yours has more patches than my trousers. You're young."

"I'm telling you, I'm twenty-four!"

"And I'm telling you you're not. I do not do business with children."

"I'll be eighteen in two weeks."

Failure isn't an option. Azrael needs this, he won't go back until he obtains what he came for. He has braved the storm, tolerated the cold and done despicable things - too much work has been put into this to just give up.

"Come back in two weeks, then."

"In two weeks, your business will be of no use to me. I don't have time to spare."

Mercer pauses. He is intrigued, Azrael can tell. Curiosity is nagging at him, begging him to agree like a dog begs for food.

"What's your name kid?"

"Azrael."

"Follow me, Azrael."

They slalom between carpets, foulards and curtains to find a door. It creaks open, revealing the back of the shop. Wooden flooring gives way to stone and cloth, with shelves of jars brushing the ceiling. Opaque liquids float in their glass prisons, looking for a way out like fish in an aquarium.

Souls. Lives.

The two are inextricably linked in most cases anyway: people hardly ever succeeded in capturing just one.

"What are you looking for exactly?"

"I need a life."

"That much I guessed. What kind?"

"A girl's, aged nine."

The jars' liquids seem to quiver as Mercer's calloused hands reach out towards them and Azrael swears he can hear whines ricocheting off the glass as they close around one, extirpating it from its shelf.

"How about this one?"

"I need a life without a soul."

"It's an unusual request."

"I'm an unusual guy."

Mercer's eyes narrow to slits, hidden by eyebrows that crease with concentration. The hostage is returned to its place on the shelf - fingertips ghost over the ranks of glass, as a hum tumbles from the trader's lips.

"Give me a second, I know it's here somewhere…ah, here we go. Female; nine; was brought in a couple of weeks ago."

The liquid inside the jar lacks both the vitality and opaqueness of the other substances and for a moment Azrael wonders if Mercer is trying to trick him, but it's just an instant- it's a risk he needs to take.

"Perfect, how much do you charge for it?"

He fumbles insides his pockets to produce his wallet. Several notes are already pinched between his fingertips when the shopkeeper raises his hand.

"Human lives are nothing money can buy."-Azrael's heartbeat accelerates as he holds his breath- "A life for a life, that's my price."

It was to be expected.

"Seems like a fair bargain. Would this one do?"

It takes him a moment to free the first vial from his bag but before long it is resting in the palm of his hand, extended towards Mercer ready for him to possess. The man's lips twist in a knowing grin – tangled locks whip the air as he shakes his head.

"That won't do boy. A human life isn't worth a cat's."

"You said a life for a life."

"I did, but not all lives are worth the same."

Azrael grits his teeth. He had hoped Mercer would settle for a smaller price. Souls and Lives are a lucrative business - he would have happily sacrificed the lesser items of his loot for the purchase and sold his most prized ones elsewhere.

"I can offer the life of a man."

He holds out a second vial.

"A homeless, old man. That life isn't worth a young girl's."

"But it's a human life."

"His life had little potential left. Hers was full of it - she could have achieved much had she lived, she could have gone to school, had children… that increases the price."

He doesn't realize he is biting the inside of his cheek until blood reaches his taste buds. He has a single vial left.

"This is my last offer."

Mercer picks it up. The glass is stained red- it had been a sloppy, hurried job that made a bigger mess than Azrael had initially planned. He examines it carefully, mouthing his conclusions beneath his breath.

"Female; 40; No children; Single. Not bad."

"Will you accept it as payment?"

"No. Not enough child-baring potential to make up for the girl's."

Fuck. No. No. No. He needs that life…he's desperate for it. He cannot go back without it; he can't bear to go back without it. There has to be something he can do, anything at all.

"Sir, I need that life. I'll do anything to pay for it"

He has to bite back tears of frustration. He can't be pathetic, not now. Mercer pauses, yanks the young man's chin upwards – Azrael can feel his nails digging into his flesh but doesn't dare move. He is too scrawny to win a fight.

"I've seen you before haven't I? It's been bothering me since the moment you stepped foot in my shop. Have you been here before? …or maybe you live in the area? …wait, no, you were in the papers two days ago, you're the brother of the lass who fell in the Thames."

Azrael jerks his head free, massaging his jaw where nails have cut skin.

"So what if I am, what difference does it make to you?"

"You want a life to bring your sister back don't you?"

"She had been dead for hours when they pulled her out, no one was there to catch her life and soul when they left. The cold preserved the body, if I find a life to infuse it with I'm hoping the soul will come back to it. They do that sometimes."

"Oh I'm aware. Souls tend to like things they're familiar with."

Mercer toys with the vial still in his hand, his expression impossible to decipher as he keeps his eyes locked on Azrael. The silence is driving him mad. Thump. Thump. Thump. Seconds seem minutes, spelled out by each beating of his heart.

"The woman. You took her life didn't you?"

"I collected it, yes."

"No, not collected. You took it, forcibly. You left blood stains on the vial."

"I was desperate."

Thump. Thump. Thump. Say something. Please say something.

"I like you Azrael, you've got guts. Not many people are willing to kill to procure lives and souls to sell."

"I do what I need to."

A smile tugs at the corners of Mercer's lips- there is something almost predatory about it that makes the hair stand on the nape of the young man's neck. Thump. Thump. Thump.

"You can have the life…"

Azrael can already taste victory, "…if you accept to work for me. I need someone to collect my merchandise by all means possible: this godforsaken science is making people far too healthy, and if we wait for people to die naturally there will be shortages."

Azrael's face falls at these words.

"You want me to be responsible for people's deaths?"

"Exactly."

What gives him the authority to decide people's fate? What gives him authority to cut someone's life short? It is one thing to kill once out of despair and necessity, it is another to do so repeatedly and in cold blood. Doing such things has repercussions, leaves deep scars on a person's soul impossible to erase. Yet he needs that girl's life- it is his best chance at having his sister back. How many lives is his sister's worth? He doesn't know. He doesn't care. Strangers' lives are a currency - tokens to be traded, that's all.

"I accept."

"Excellent."

DARK EYES
Johnny Raspin

Now I lay me down to sleep,
I pray the Lord my soul to keep,
If I should die before I wake,
I pray the Lord my soul to take.

Many children are expected to recite this each evening, after supper and before they are tucked into bed. The sentiment is true enough, may the Lord indeed protect everyone as they enter into the clutches of the night. A simple prayer that drips from the mouths of trusting children also rings out in varied measure from the hearts of any person who is flung into darkness as they lay down to sleep. But, is the darkness really any different from the light? Surely everything remains the same. This is what the many tell themselves to abate their credulous minds. Of course it is nonsense, light and darkness are so obviously different in the benefits and dangers they present; however, they do surprisingly share some similarities regarding hazards. You most certainly have heard that one should never look directly at the sun, for the simple reason that its radiance will blind you, but have you ever heard, or do you know, that it is dangerous in equal measure to stare into the dark? Perhaps everyone does and that is why, whether you admit it or not, you ask for protection when your head hits the pillow.

Once there was a young girl who became infatuated with the magical possibilities that the darkness' blank canvas offered her imagination. But danger awaited her, for just as the darkness shrouds in shadows all it touches, so do the lines between imagination and reality often become indistinguishable in its presence.

An empty closet existed within the living room of Chillingham orphanage. It was completely devoid of light and, although in reality it was only a few feet in depth, the darkness gave off the illusion that the closet's interior was vast. Unlike most children who would flee from the terrifying possibilities that the darkness can offer, in to the sanctity of sleep, Nina would allow her eyes to wander within. It could be said that she had dark eyes. Eyes that glimmered with the unusual joy of the dark, rather than the light.

The best nights were when the moon was undercover and the street lamps were yet unlit. It was on these nights that Nina, with the assistance of candlelight, would sneak downstairs and enter the living room, mindful not to stand on the floorboards that she knew creaked. Her steady hand would reach and open the closet door, the beating of her heart at this savoured point would become quicker and quicker. Anticipation grew with each inch the door opened. Darkness would spill from the closet, begging to envelop her, pleading for her to extinguish the candle.

She would hear the musings of fairies, the laughter of children from far away places; she could smell exotic fruit that grew on undiscovered plants and trees, and feel the warm breath of a creature much larger than herself. All she had to do was blow out the candle and relinquish the last tether that held her to this world. So, with a single breath Nina would banish the light, extinguishing the hinderance it had on her imagination, and would fearlessly gaze into the closet, awaiting new wonders that she knew would find her.

The frequency of Nina's dark, visual meanderings increased. It reached the point where the young girl spent so much time fixing her eyes on the darkness of the closet that light in general became quite abhorrent, and painful to her eyes. It was becoming unhealthy. Very rarely would she venture outside and when she did, it was only after every inch of her skin had been shielded from the light. Darkness was what brought her joy, whilst simultaneously being the cause of her growing physical and mental ailments.

Depressive moods would afflict Nina. Her eyes grew darker and her skin paler. The only comfort she drew from the day's brightness was knowing that it had an end. The light was what she needed, but she withdrew further and further away, because it was the dark that won her heart.

Nina's quest to delve deeper into the dark closet led to one final look into the black. She had indeed developed a remarkable ability to glimpse things that no other eye could see, but in certain situations it is often more beneficial not to obtain the ability of sight. It may have been the young lady's fearlessness when trudging through the night that allowed her to create where other's would flee; or conversely, and horrifically so, her fearlessness could have been the very factor that enabled her to view things that actually existed within the dark closet. It may well have been this fearlessness that attracted a variety of creatures.

This princess of the night looked disdainfully at the candle as she navigated her way downstairs. If it was a certainty that her path would be clear, then she would have blown the candle out right then and there, but it was not, so she begrudgingly allowed it to assist. Nina, like so many nights before, arrived at the closet and, filled with expectation, she reached for the handle and gently opened the door. The darkness tumbled out and attempted to engulf Nina only to be stopped by the candlelight. It hovered around the young girl… waiting. Nina could hear it moaning, weeping, as the closet held her gaze. It was different; the merriment of the fairies, the laughter of children, the sweet scent of fruit, the warm breath of creatures much larger than her, were vacant. Instead, as the darkness filled Nina's eyes and its groans fed into her ears, dozens of shadowy hands reached out from the closet and pulled her near.

For the first time Nina felt the beginnings of fear, but she did not struggle against the hands. Never before had her imaginings taken on such physicality, never before had they been able to lead her so forcefully. Previously, Nina could not understand why people were frightened of the dark; after all, it served to perpetuate the most vivid fantasies. However, she quickly realised that these were not figments of her imagination.

The darkness continued to pull her forward, slowly devouring her.

It was a breath that blew out the candle, but not one that came from the young girl's lungs. This was vile, rotten, undeniably from a thing with blackened caps for teeth; that had mould growing on its tongue and infected spittle running down its chin. The orange tip of the wick went black like everything else, leaving only smoke that momentarily brought relief from putrid breath. It was too dark to see anything, but she could hear and smell something new. Blood gargling. The thing's breath was cold and moist, it clung to the skin and caused it to itch. It felt as though the remnants of phlegm moved like tiny insects across Nina's cheeks. It was close now. Screaming was futile, for the hands covered her mouth and reduced the girl's cries to mere mumbles. They grasped tighter… pulled harder… until a new pair of bony, rough hands grasped Nina by the throat. The closet door slowly shut and a cackle rang out in the absolute darkness.

Nina was not present at breakfast.

*

Nina never spoke to anyone about her affiliation with the darkness. Perhaps she felt that the other children would think her strange. After all, it is hard for such a person to find friends when their desires are so… abnormal. Nevertheless, it is an ironic injustice that a child so unnoticed in life only became noticed when they vanished. The carers at Chillingham orphanage looked high and low for Nina, but their searches, no matter how thorough, were fruitless. The only inkling of her whereabouts was a melted trail of candle wax that lead from the bottom of the stairs into the living room. There, it seemed to gather into a heap outside of the closet, before resuming its journey under the gap of the door. The carers followed this path. They hesitantly opened the closet door, expecting to find Nina, but there was nothing—the trail vanished a mere foot inside…

The next cause of action was to inform the authorities and hope that they could assist, but this caused nothing but condemnation to rain down upon Chillingham. The media began to comment on the incapability of the staff to keep the unfortunates safe. Rumours began to circulate about a child murderer that lurked in their midst, and a full investigation was launched into the whereabouts of Nina. It was then that the visitations happened. Many of the children claimed to have seen Nina in their dreams, there were even times when individuals awoke to see her at the end of their bed, pleading for them to search for her. Save me from the witch, she chases me deeper into the dark. The children were hushed and told to keep their imaginings to themselves. With little progress and the safety of other children in question, it was decided that Chillingham should be closed and the occupants dispersed to different orphanages.

As the years passed the building fell into disrepair; it became a ghost of its former self and parallel to its reduction ran the growth of superstition surrounding Nina's disappearance. This resulted in the legend of the Chillingham witch coming into existence.

It is said that if a person stands outside the orphanage as the sun sinks into the horizon and then they close their eyes and listen as darkness descends, the sound of children reciting a prayer can be heard:

Now I lay me down to sleep,
I pray the Lord my soul to keep,
If I should die before I wake,
I pray the Lord my soul to take.

Once the prayer is finished and the listener does not flee in fear, but rather gazes through the living room window, then they will see Nina, standing with candle in hand, in front of the closet door. If the brave onlooker gently speaks, it need not be louder than a whisper... Nina... The young girl will turn, and as the candle light illuminates her face, a state of dread will flood their soul. Hairs stand on end, one after another in an almost rhythmical fashion; shivers travel up the spine to the beat of helplessness...

The fear that her distorted features portray, the streams of terror that run down her face, is an image that evokes feelings of pain, for it unravels and stands wholly against the natural desire to keep children safe. Many try and rush to help, but as soon as they entertain this thought, she is pulled by some invisible force, swept up and dragged through the closet door, and as she disappears, candle and all, they are left gazing, waiting, praying... again they gently call, Nina...

It may be the Lord's responsibility to keep children safe as they delve into sleep, but it is mankind's responsibility to partake in their safety when they are awake.

The luring darkness will entice their impressionable hearts and if there is one thing that you take from this narrative, let it be that witches do indeed hide in every closet, and that it is not wise to stare into the dark.

THE LOVELIES SIN
Beth Reeves

Cox

"Blackmail," his voice squeaked down the crackling phone line. "Everything I have. They want it all, and if they don't get it, they'll go after Lana."

"You can't think who it might be? Got to be a reason they're after you Campbell, who've you pissed off lately?" I probed.

I downed a mouthful of whiskey; Harry said he'd got my name off a friend. Someone who used to be a cop until something went down, and they pinned it on him. Went from Midtown to Harlem. I must've met him in his past life.

"I came home to find a note under my door. It was typed, telling me they wanted $1000. And if I didn't give it to them, I'd never see her again. They're coming to collect. They been watchin' us, watchin' her, they really could get to her. You need to understand, she's all I got," his voice became strained, like he was holding back tears.

I pulled a cigarette out of its packet and settled it between my lips.

"And you have that kind of money? How'd you become a target Harry, flashing your cash?"

"I didn't mean to. I won it playing cards, me and Ron were down Frank's on 129th. I couldn't believe it, bought drinks for everyone in the room I was so happy. Just my luck really. I thought I could turn my life around. Get a nicer place, get Lana a big ring. Now this."

I thrust the tip of the cigarette into the flame of a match and inhaled. Red embers glowed as they chased their way up its length. I filled the room with smoke before I smirked, "Well, that's somewhere to start. Bet Frank didn't fancy being cleaned out by a rookie."

He gulped.

"What's your address Harry? I'll come over tonight." Scrawling 121st and Park down on a scrap of paper, I hung up.

*

Ron
"Won't you be a doll and grab the money? I need to clean up."

She wore patent ivory heels and sleek, shining stockings that hugged her legs. They were arranged to be looked at. One calf draped lightly over the other knee. Her dress was red, crimson and tight, a bold siren. It had torn up the thigh in the commotion and lay across her lap, leaving little to the imagination. One hand hung loosely over legs, her fingernails were sharp and traced lulling circles around the bright, puckered wound on her knee. The blood had already begun to congeal, but the bruise looked strangely alluring on her porcelain skin. Her shoulders were relaxed, her head titled to one side. Her mouth was a tight line, pulled over sharp pearly teeth. Darks eyes set deep in her face, with no emotion. They were empty. Her mouth formed the shapes of words that didn't escape her pursed lips; a frown creased her forehead.

"Oh, look what you made me do Harry, you should have let that silly girl alone, I thought I meant more to you than this," her gaze rested on the body as she toyed with her hair and wiped a bead of sweat off her brow.

I couldn't read her face but she still had that look in her eye, and I began to contemplate whether I'd end up the same way as her husband. Slumped back on his knees like he was praying or still begging for her forgiveness. His insides on the outside. A harsh laugh erupted from her wide mouth and the sound reverberated through me. I couldn't keep my eyes off her body. The torn dress, her heaving chest. Her wide, half-lidded eyes, her lashes caressing her high cheekbones. I strode across the room, my foot knocking Harry's head lolling on his shoulders, and I grabbed her. I needed her like the devil needed sin.

*

Cox
The dim streets were slick with the recent rain and the Coupe's tires streaked the pavements with murky water. I passed Harry Campbell's building on the right, slow, so that I could gauge the entrance, but not slow enough that it would draw attention. There wasn't a doorman. It looked expensive, but then so did the women who stood bedraggled on the corner, cocking their hips and calling out to men. I turned around the block, cut the lights, and parked a few

buildings back on the opposite side of the road. I lit a cigarette and dragged on it until my lungs burned. The smoke drifted in front of my eyes making the buildings on the street blur at the edges. The light was on in Campbell's apartment and I could see the silhouettes of two people in the window. The one shaped like a woman stepped closer to the window frame and drew the curtain, sealing the light behind it and leaving an orange glow around its edge. I reached in to the glove compartment and grabbed the whiskey, downing a mouthful and then another, waiting for it to warm me. I sunk a little deeper into my seat and set myself up for the wait.

The rain had begun to bounce off the roof of the car again before the door of the apartment building swung open. Campbell's light had gone out. The door bounced shut again, as though the people behind it couldn't decide whether to step out into the glare of the streetlights. I slipped out of the car and shut the door slowly, its click almost inaudible. Crossing the street, the rain soaked through to my shoulders, but its echo was a good cover. As I reached the steps of the building, the figures were muttering under their breath in the doorway. My hand instinctively went to my waist, checking my gun was there, a colt .38 detective special. I stayed in the shadows until they left, the rain pelting my face like bullets. I had to move swiftly to catch the door before it swung shut.

The foyer was large and dim; it was late and quiet. The far wall was lined with pigeonholes, several of them had letters and The New York Times hanging out of them, while others looked thick with dust. The light in the centre of the ceiling flickered intermittently, illuminating the stairway on the left. Campbell was four floors up. Number 127. I paused outside it, doors lined both walls and the mahogany frames were numbered with golden plaques. A muffled radio could be heard behind one of them and a deep voice down the hall was shouting. Yet, only a loud silence escaped Campbell's apartment. I pressed my ear to Campbell's door and it gave way, not having been pulled shut properly. I waited to see if I had disturbed anyone inside. I didn't know how many people were in the apartment. With my hand on my gun I nudged the door open with my foot. The room was in darkness. My eyes blinked as they tried to adjust and my hand brushed the wall searching for the light switch. When I found it, my eyes were struck by two things: the flood of light and the dead body on the floor.

A bitter perfume lingered in the stale air. Against the far wall, beneath the window I had looked in from the street, stood a mahogany sideboard with a sliding glass door, housing crystal tumblers. An ornate silver tray sat on top with a matching crystal decanter filled with an amber liquid. A single glass stood discarded next to it, crimson lipstick marked the rim. On the right, a half partition wall divided the lounge and the kitchen. A pastel blue fridge occupied the far, left corner and on the right, a very clean, off-white oven stood looking as though it had never been used. Dark smears of fresh blood marked the walls, and a dirty, blood-clotted rag lay crumpled on the floor.

Campbell's body lay awkwardly, the bright yellow plush rug below it was matted with blood. He was only a small man, about 5'5 – I'd guessed as much from his voice. Both of his hands were clutched at his stomach, as though he was laughing so hard he couldn't catch his breath. As I stepped closer, I realised he'd been trying to hold himself together. Huge wounds were carved into his torso, I could count at least fifteen distinct holes that gawped like angry mouths. His heart had been pierced twice and his intestines had escaped the confines of his body through the lacerations in his middle. His trousers were marked with a dark, wet stain. So frightened, he'd pissed himself. The pungent smell mixed with the perfume of fresh blood. His eyes were bloodshot and bulging, frozen in a glassy stare. He had a thick moustache, that was a shade or two darker than the greying hair on his head. Blood had choked him in his final attempts at breath, leaving his teeth a sickly copper hue. His jugular had been severed, showering blood over himself and whoever had killed him. The motherf— gave him no mercy.

*

Ron

The rain bombarded the dim street. Nothing seemed to be able to cut through the darkness for long, not even the waning streetlights. A permanent cloud hung over this part of Harlem, far from the glistening world of Manhattan, the grey streets imposed on each other, the people did not. The vermin that lived on these streets trampled over the first person who started to look like they could escape. Like rats caught in a metal pipe, you put a fire up their ass and they'll tear their way through a brick wall. Harlem wasn't a place for big dreams, only pipe dreams, and people find that out pretty quickly. Girls with long hair and short skirts stuck their arms with junk, so that they could live out their Hollywood dreams without realising they never got past the Hudson River.

I walked with purpose, Lana sauntered. The click of her heels against the hard, black street echoed off the faces of the buildings. No one who saw us took any notice; we were nothing to no one, except Harry Campbell, but we didn't need to worry about him anymore. Lana swung the black briefcase by her side like it was the Fourth of July. I guess it was, for her. She turned to face me, stopping to grab my face.

"Don't worry baby, I know he rang that PI you told him about. I heard him on the phone, told him all about that note I left. Nearly crying even! They won't be looking our way. He'll think it was one of Frank's goons, come to get this money back."

Her melodic voice soothed my frayed wits. She stroked my temple, her fingertips like feathers. There was still a faint metallic smell on them, still blood under her nails. The rain battered our faces, smearing her makeup. Her hair was a tangled mess, plastered to her face like serpents. Her dark eyes looked up into mine and I saw nothing in them. But like magnets, our lips collided, mashing herself into me. She bit down hard on my lips, blood gushing into our mouths, mixing with the sweet, relentless rain. She was an animal, with a taste for blood and my heart was racing when she pushed me away. I craved more.

"Let's not miss our train, baby," she drawled the last word out of her cherry-stained lips. My fingers quickly touched my mouth; I winced. My lip had begun to swell already. Yet, my eyes had not left hers and blindly, my feet took off after her. We jogged down towards the underpass that led to the station platform. It was darker here than the rest of Harlem, there were no streetlights. It was a hiding place for shadows and those who needed disappear.

PEARS
Ellie Reeves

A stripy sock and a chicken wing sit in guilty silence
I am the sock and you are the wing
We come as a pair, that much is obvious
As we sit on the sofa with a pot of tea.
My parents, two Maracas named Stephanie and Hayden,
Are in disdain.
The nosy Pair Of Eyes next door caught us
Making out in the alleyway and phoned to inform them of our
Disgrace.
Our casual drink in the Earrings' Bar was rudely
Interrupted by their loud preferences –
Apparently the Double Glazing's darling Red Sock would be
A better fit,
They spit beans at me until they're lightheaded.
In the light of day, their big mouths are sugar cubes
Bobbing about in the steaming tea. I wait.
We've finished the bowl of nibbles,
Your feathers are tickling my threads as they quiver rather indiscreetly.
My mother remarks that we've finished the bowl of nibbles
My father shakes his Maraca head and goes to fetch more.
To break the tension you joke
I could murder some chicken nuggets,
But I don't think they get it.

AND I FEEL TO BE A COG IN SOMETHING TURNING
George Rennison

It takes a long time for the sun to start setting set on Friday July 23rd. The sickening intensity of its burn peaks and starts to tail away at quarter past seven in the evening. This is when the festival's West Stage has turned its ears to the crisp snatch of a licked snare drum, to the melting fug of thick amplified keys; to the sound of The Roots.

The floor vibrates with pulsing bass and the soles of your shoes are on fire. Thick green boots with a full wedge heel, killer style. You stand at the edge of the makeshift platform, adjust your beige mohair jacket, watch the band riff and sway and groove their song to the finish line. Questie slams hard on the cymbals. The crowd goes berserk. In an attempt to dampen the jolt of fear that shoots through you, again, you adjust your jacket.

You nod to the roadie wearing headphones that clamp his hair at an awkward angle. A foam band connects the two ears, and it's saturated with damp sweat. It is July. White guy in a black t-shirt? Roast turkey. He shuffles past you with a grin, trips himself over in his dusty sneakers, and dashes down the steps to the greenroom out back. He'll ring his girlfriend in a daze. "Dude!" he'll scream down his cell "I just met Erykah Badu."

He did. You are Erykah Badu.

From where you're standing, the scaffold poles supporting the West Stage obscure your view of the crowd, but you got a good look on the way in. The space packed with bodies piled upon bodies; sweating, sunburnt, naked. White guys in no t-shirts? Raw turkey. In the gap between songs, the sound of the mob resurges. The shouts and screams mesh into a forceful energy that ebbs and flows up to the raised stage. Like a wave on the shore at the beach.

You picture a beach. The sun's bright gleam. You walk beside your son, bare feet on the hot sand. He's only just old enough to balance himself upright. He still needs your palm wrapped round his tiny, stubby fingers, hand to hand, teaching him how to put one foot in front of the other.

You rub your belly where he used to kick, as if he is still inside you. It was only moments ago, surely. Not two years. It was only moments ago that you were a happy family.

You gulp. Panic floods your body.

You're fretting he may turn out just like his Dad, and that that's too bad, and that here's nothing you can do about that. And you're confused and you're trying to move on, but when you look into his eyes, you see the smiling guy he came from. Rolling his hips to your song in a club, and taking you home and showing you love. Treating your mama like a real Dallas queen; it seems like a dream all the things that you've seen. And it breaks your heart 'cos there's still respect, but it's messy and bruised and things don't connect. And you wonder if you even know the meaning of real, as you stop and say no, and you break off the deal. Bask in the glare of the sun's bright gleam. Forget what it was all meant to mean.

"Imma bring out a friend of mine for this one right here, can I do that?"

Tariq snaps you back, you have a job to do. The Queen of Neo-Soul, they call you. You can't be nervous. You start walking. Elegant stride, poised, ready. Keep it together. He's announcing the special guest, but you don't feel all that special.

"Put your hands together ladies and gentlemen…"

The stage is long, and takes a long time to cross, but you reach your checkpoint. The mic. Not your mic. The black cylinder protrudes from the top of the stand, ugly and unfamiliar.

"Y'all not ready…"

He's hyping up the crowd, but it's you who's not ready. Not ready to make that second record you've been putting off all year. Not ready to raise your kid on your own. Not ready to lose how you made your man laugh. You stand in a daze, a million miles away, as screams and shouts drift in the air, the heat of the crowd palpable.

"… for Miss E Badu."

A surge of howls at the sound of your name. The name you chose.

Badu. To manifest truth and light. It swamps you, it makes you feel twelve years old, sitting; arms folded, legs crossed on the couch. This ain't my name. Your mama's jaw slack, full-blown taken aback. This is a slave name. She stops you there, she'll hear no more. Don't you say that. Did the white man give you that name? Erica is a beautiful name. You jump off the couch and leave the room, she doesn't understand. And you don't want to change your name, it's not that. You just wanna find meaning in it. So you do. Kah. The inner self. Remember how in school one day you learnt you were inferior, remember how you felt the day you first started your period. Remember how you searched and found your name in the interior.

Well. Remembering is good if you don't let it be the fear of you.

You wonder if your son'll be as stubborn as you, or if he could ever be anything but that. You are his mother, after all. You wonder if he'll choose himself a name. You wonder if he'll carve it deep into himself. You hope so.

You raise your arm, step to the mic, and start to sing.

Cautious, tentative. Finding your feet. Healing takes a while. But the beat kicks in, you bop back and you're off. It's a sad song. But maybe you sing it for Seven. Baby, don't worry, you know that you got me…

The band roll through the verse, spitting words in a rap that blurs in sonic intricacy. It's not your turn to sing anymore, and as you close your mouth and breathe through your nose, you start to look at the crowd for the first time. The field is teeming with people. They have no idea what you are going through. Maybe some of them have no idea who you are. Just a blissed out black woman in a headwrap. You walk a little circle.

The mic stand is too low. Typical. You're tall, especially in those heels. You fumble for the knob that'll lift it, raise it up to meet you. But the cord of the mic is tangled, looping it tight around the stand.

You lift the mic, careful not to knock the whole thing over. It's coming up, your second chorus. You'd better unwind it quick. And don't pull it too taut, or it'll pop out at the base. And you'll be singing, but nothing'll pick up and no one'll be able to hear you.

You find the best way is to pass the mic under the stand with one hand, into the other hand and over the top. Hand to hand. Over and under. Bop a little, look casual, look like you're in control.

You turn to Tariq. His mic cable is fully unravelled, it sprawls across the stage into a long, snaking wreath. He tilts the mic down into his mouth casually, the way the boys do. That's how your Andre does it. You try to put him out of your mind, but it's like everywhere you look there's a piece of him. It's a daily task, putting him out of your mind.

And then you spot it, maybe. There's an inflatable beach ball, drifting through the sky, bouncing off the white palms stretching up, out of the crowd.

And you're back on the beach with Seven. Hand to hand. Sun's bright gleam. Hot sand wrinkling your toes, and he giggles as the water crashes over his ankles. But you're not afraid anymore. Don't know if it's the relief that the mic is yours now, that it'll follow you across the stage wherever you strut. Don't know if it's the song, as you echo Tariq's that shit don't matter and mean it. But you feel lighter. You feel like you could…

The mic cable snags. It's caught on the front of the stage. But you're cool now, you make it a turn, and you throw in your old hook off your debut: Rimshot! You remember sitting in a basement flat in Philly, with these very same boys, finishing off those first ever demos, signing off your first ever record, your roots. Huh. The crowd laps up your little reference. They do know who you are.

Bolstered, you go to Tariq for the chorus. Pretend like you're his girl in the story of the song. Get up close and curl your fingers round his shoulders seductively. It's cool, he's your brother. But there's something so naughty, exhilarating. You haven't touched too many guys since Mr Benjamin. Yeah, but the future is yours, girl.

You strut as Questie's tapping picks up again, and add a few da, daaas to the middle eight. In your element. Relaxed and loose and…

The mic feeds back, a warbling screech through the speakers. Shit. What is this? You can't help but think to yourself if it's like karma coming back to bite you. You are a pisces. A pisces in pieces.

That beach ball rolls your way again, the sun refracting through its plastic coating in a trickle of colour. Like the tints of sun-filled coral blue, the stained glass spilling across the old wooden pews, washing your back as you kneel in your best pink Sunday shoes. The days when your voice was still learning it could sing. Your mum is sad, your Dad has walked out. How you covered your ears as they'd bicker and shout. And all her anger and disappointment hits you now, and you understand you'll get through somehow. It's like a kick in the stomach. It's like Seven kicks you in the stomach. As if he's still inside you. And you realise everything in that moment. He'll always be inside you.

You continue singing. Persevere. Only more than that now, you're determined. Questie's snare taps pick up again in frantic, building semiquavers, and you throw a taunting get up, y'all! C'mon, y'all! at the crowd. It's just you and the band. You and the boys. And you feel to be a cog in something turning alright.

Here we go, there's nothing stopping you now. The music growing, the crowd leaning in, digging deep. You let out an animal yowl, it jumps from your throat. You hold it, wobbling uncontrollably through a cascade of notes. Aaah. Higher. Aaah yaaah. Foot stamping. Aaah yaaah. Arm raised to the sky. Higher still. And then a scream; primal, wild. Letting it all exude from your body in an exorcism of song.

You are blessed, Erykah.

The Legendary Roots Crew and Erykah Badu.

What a day, what a day, what a day.

21 DAYS
Saskia Reynolds

1.

"All I'm saying, right, is that if the supermarkets have started selling milk made from nuts, is life really worth living?"

We've been on the road for approximately three hours and fifty minutes. And for approximately three hours and fifty minutes I have been prey to the commentary of the delightfully backwards Saoirse Gillian Moore. A stranger who, until this afternoon, I would not have known likes eating Kit-Kats in the same way I imagine a totalitarian dictator would: by biting all the chocolate off first. I suppose I shouldn't be surprised. What can you expect from a hitchhiker, if not abhorrent eating etiquette?

"I'm wondering that about now," I mutter.

I see Saoirse look at me out of the corner of my eye. She considers me for a moment, then sighs, pulls her knees up to her chest and turns to stare out of the window.

"Yeah, I guess you're right," she mumbles. "We've all got bigger fish to fry." Pause. "You married?"

I try to hide my wince. "No."

Saoirse's face lights up with a terrifying grin. "You hesitated! Ex-husband? Did he leave you for someone else? Did he run away with some beach body model?" Her dreamy expression is disrupted by a theatrical gasp. "Did you cheat on h-?"

"No- look, stop it, alright? We've known each other for all of three hours - you don't know me and I don't know you, so let's just drop it, alright? You don't see me asking you about your love life."

"Well-"

"That wasn't an invitation."

We settle back into an uneasy silence. Only Joni Mitchell's now uncomfortably mellow guitar riffs can be heard over the hum of the engine. "At least tell me your name. I told you mine; it's not fair for you to have leverage over me when I have none over you."

"Leverage? I didn't ask you what your name was, you just told me. And I'm playing your CD - I don't have to tell you anything I don't want to." Saoirse narrows her eyes at me. "You're quite impolite."

I turn my attention back to the road. A lorry driver speeds past on my right. Behind it I see the northbound lane is jammed. Unusual. There must be some big event going on in London.

"It's Nora," I say, reaching to turn the CD player off. "And I've had enough of Joni for now." I ignore my passenger's sulking expression, though can't help but wonder how such a loud-mouthed hitchhiker wound up on the side of a main road with only a rucksack on her back.
And then I turn on the radio.

5.
"Holy shit! What the fuck, what the fuck, what the fuck, what the-"

"Saoirse! Calm. Down."

"How can I calm down? I just shot someone!"

"You don't know that!"

"Uh, yeah I fucking do!"

"How?"

*

I didn't see her pick up the gun. I was taking a pee break and when I was done I turned around to see Saoirse standing in front of me with a pistol in her hands.

"Look what I found!" she exclaimed, half-laughing. She held it out to show me.

"That is...indeed...a firearm."

"Do you reckon someone dropped it when they were making a getaway?"

"I don't know," I said, still staring at the gun. "We aren't exactly near any major banks or vaults so it seems unlikely. A hunter, maybe. We are in the middle of a field, there's bound to be a load of pheasants around here." My brain couldn't keep up with the words coming out of my mouth.

"More like flesh-eating zombies." She held it out in front of her and shut one eye as she concentrated on nothing. She was definitely ignoring the panic on my face.

"Is it loaded?" I asked.

"I don't know. Let's find out."

Before I could even try and stop her, the atomic bomb did indeed go off.

Saoirse Gillian Moore killed everyone. I had nothing to do with it.

*

Once I have the gun and the ringing in my ears is quieter, the shrieking lowers in pitch.

"You're not screaming anymore," I whisper.

"No. I gathered that."

"Then who is?"

The answer to our question comes in the form of a loud yell, and a red-skinned man in a stretched white tank top and cargo shorts walking out of his house, that we only now see, has a gaping hole through one of the ground floor windows. He's got a hunting rifle in his left hand.

Saoirse lowers the pistol back to the ground. "At least I didn't shoot anyone," she whispers.

"Run. Seriously. Fucking run. Right now!"

1.

"I didn't even know meteor showers were a thing. I guess that's what happens when you don't have a 'permanent residence'. No one bothers to buy you a radio... or an encyclopedia."

We've pulled over. I'm still staring at the cars on the northbound lane, all pushed up against each other. I wouldn't be surprised if the metal railing started to bend from the pressure of having all those cars rammed up against it.

And then I look at the passengers.

There's a woman with her phone pressed to her ear, crying. She's alone. Then there's a guy behind her in an Audi wearing a suit. But he's also crying and threading some sort of bracelet through his fingers.

The rain starts to pour down. Fat drops bang against the roof.

Saoirse turns the volume up on the radio. We listen in silence.

12.

Saoirse is curled up by the fire; the blanket I put around her shoulders is still hanging over her. She fell asleep looking over old photo albums, and laughing at pictures of me as a baby.

The sky's ominous golden tint has spread further and is now looming above our heads.

I look out the window towards the trees in the distance. I can see mum's headstone. It's surrounded by wildflowers. The little blue ones.

2.

The car broke down.

Saoirse doesn't have any money and I only have a debit card that is about thirty pounds away from just being a piece of plastic.

We left the car somewhere off of the M6. Conveniently, it decided to give up near enough to a service station that we ditched it and trekked through the adjacent field to get there.

And now Saoirse Gillian Moore and I are lying on a stiff, unforgiving Premier Inn mattress, in the middle of the night, in stunned silence. Is it really the end of the world? Is this how I die? On a cheap mattress next to a mysterious homeless seventeen-year old who likes Joni Mitchell?

I imagine my mum her in her house. Maybe she'd be happy. Maybe she wouldn't have heard the news yet - she'd only turn it on at 6 pm every night. Maybe she'd be fine. Hopefully she'd just be enjoying the sea, like always.

I feel Saoirse stirring next to me. I turn to see her eyes staring into mine. I turn onto my back.

"I'm going to Dover," she says. "That's near enough to Eastbourne, isn't it?"

"Do you have family there?"

"No, not really."

"Quick getaway trip before the earth implodes, then?"

"Exactly! I've never been to France before."

There's a crack in the ceiling, right above my head. It looks like a tree branch.
"Do you not get on with your family, then?" I ask.

Silence.

"I don't really have one. My parents left me when I was little."

"I'm sorry."

"But what about you? What about your secret love life?"

I sigh in defeat and turn back to her. "Fine," I say. "I'll tell you three things and no more because I will not cry in front of you. One: she had green eyes. Two: I had loved her since I was seventeen. Three: she love me so she slept with someone else."

6.

We pass the hours spent walking by keeping each other company. Saoirse tells me about living in foster homes.

"I really thought I could be someone's daughter, you know? But then eventually you realise that they can't ever love you properly. You're always temporary. And then when you run out of cuteness and a general lack of accountability suddenly you're not very marketable. No one wants a teenager if they haven't been able to enjoy it's pre-adolescent innocence. I'm damaged goods... what's the fun in that?"

11.

It's odd coming back to a place you know so well yet can hardly remember. I remember driving down this road, the smell of the sea getting stronger with every second. Now I find that my voice, talking about walking along the cliffs, licking ice creams and trying not to get it all in my hair, has replaced my mother's.

"My parents don't live here anymore," I say to Saoirse as we turn onto the private road that leads to the bungalow. "I just wanted to be here. It was my sister's birthday the day I picked you up, but...my mother and sister share the same birthday and I dislike my sister so...coming here felt like the better choice."

For once Saoirse stays quiet.

17.

I'm watching Saoirse dancing along the lawn, her arms flailing around her, and I realise that she's probably never seen the sea before. Her dancing is suddenly the most endearing thing I've seen all my life. My nostrils are filled with ocean air and I'm almost five again.

I yell her name and hold up yet another mug of hot chocolate, filled to the brim with stale marshmallows that I found tucked away in the annex store cupboard.

She runs to me gleefully.

She really is just a child.

21.

"I'm glad you didn't go to Dover. Though I don't know what you would have done there anyway. They never would have let you on a ferry without a passport."

Saoirse keeps staring out of the window, though I think I see the side of her mouth turn upwards slightly. "I guess I didn't really think it through."

"Don't worry," I say. "I know you wanted to get away from your house. I understand. For the time we have left, I'll look after you."

Saoirse's eyes look like glassy orbs. It's mildly disturbing. But then she gets up from the armchair, walks over to me and wraps her arms, dripping with sweat, around my shoulders.

"I don't know you," she says. "But I'm glad you're the person I'm going to get burnt up with."

I reciprocate, pulling her to my chest, my cheek pressed into her hair. "I think we do know each other. In fact..." I unwind her arms from around me and go over to the bottom drawer of my mother's desk - her vinyl collection - and take out Ladies Of The Canyon. I take it out of it's sleeve, suddenly feeling my mother's hands over mine, guiding them to the record player, picking up the needle, placing it where it needs to go.

"There. A parting gift," I say, looking over at Saoirse.

She's looking at me with a smile and sad eyes. The orange light coming from the sky makes her hair look like fire.

"I do love Joni," she whispers.

"I know," I reply. "She's your family, right?"

Saoirse's smile widens, like the one she gave me the first day we met.

I close my eyes--

Here comes the Big Yellow Taxi to take us away.

THE FUNERAL OF MONSIEUR HUGO
Colin Sheehan

"Dear Sir/Madam,
Please join us at the church of St Mary's Village on Friday to celebrate the life and cherish the memory of renowned Detective Pierre Hugo.
Yours faithfully,
Lady Barnett and Captain Heathfield"

In composing this brief account of the funeral of Monsieur Hugo, I thought it best to begin with the little note sent to the friends and colleagues of the great detective.

But I'm getting ahead of myself. I am Benjamin Butterford, butler to Lady Hyacinth Barnett of St Mary's Village. I have been her butler for many years now, and thought I should provide a short summary of M. Hugo's service for the probable police enquiry.

The reader will no doubt be aware of M. Hugo's untimely death, but I fear a brief summary of the facts is necessary. M. Hugo had been staying in a country house, as he often did, to recover from a nasty cold. His faithful friend Captain Heathfield had arranged for M. Hugo to stay at the house where the legend met his untimely end, stabbed in the back of the head with an undiscovered weapon. The police, as is usual in these instances, could make neither head nor tail of the case, but did manage to pair M. Hugo's death with the death of the millionaire who owned the manor. It appeared that the murderer had decided to kill the detective at the manor before their intended victim, which Captain Heathfield (quite rightly) considered "most unsporting". The poor man found himself having to arrange the particulars of what was possibly the largest funeral in the country, and so naturally, my lady leant herself to his plight.

Our connection to M. Hugo has been well documented by the press, so it will suffice to say that M. Hugo spared her ladyship considerable embarrassment in a past case. My lady has a kind heart, and it was quite within the bounds of her generosity to arrange a small gathering to be held at the grounds of her manor prior to the service at the little church. Needless to say, Captain Heathfield was overcome with gratitude and proved himself a most indispensable aid in providing details of who would be arriving.

Three such gentlemen he mentioned in passing one morning over breakfast, and I must confess on hearing their names I broke a sacred rule of British butlers and gasped. In defence for such a lapse in my duties, I can only say that it would have taken an iron will not to have exclaimed. The legendary detective Hemlock Toomes, and of course his colleague Dr Wyatt Johnson, is a man who needs no introduction, and to hear that I would be in the company of him was exceedingly thrilling. Monsieur Augustus Dupé is perhaps a little less known to some readers, but as an avid reader of detective stories, I can assure you that his mastery of the craft is every bit as good as Mr Toomes'. Indeed, the two are almost identical in their effortless skills of deduction and ratiocination. Lastly, and perhaps the least known by English readers, is Mr Philip Gunn of Los Angeles. I often find that if one has overindulged in the stories of Mr Toomes or M. Hugo (may he rest in peace), the journals of Mr Gunn provide an enlightening view of America, more than enough to prevent one from buying a ticket to the country.

Why such gentlemen were invited was never really discussed, but as any butler in a country manor can tell you, the arrival of a detective is something that should never be questioned, only assisted. As I have mentioned, I am something of a fanatic of detective works, and to hear that three such gentlemen would be present was scarce more than I could ready myself for.

The day of the service was scheduled thus: at 15:00, a light luncheon and chance for guests to meet and exchange stories of M. Hugo. At 17:00 the funeral would begin, with the service concluding at 19:00, allowing guests more time to reminisce until dinnertime at 21:00.

The day of M. Hugo's service enjoyed perfect weather. At Barnett Manor, I run a very (if I flatter myself) tight and effective ship. Everything was in perfect readiness when the guests started to arrive. Due to M. Hugo's incredible career, we were preparing for a Sultan of India, several counts and countesses of Europe, a member of our own royal family, and, of course, the three great detectives.

Consider my surprise then, when a gentleman in a trench coat, with a cocked fedora and lit cigarette, arrived in a motorcar and simply idled opposite the manor, looking at it rather ominously. He waited for so long that, forgetting my manners, I ventured from the house to enquire what he was doing. His eyes darted up to me, and when he spoke it seemed to be by forcing his words out of the corner of his mouth. "This the Barnett house?"

"Barnett Manor, sir."

"Right." He paused, relaxing his gaze back onto the house. A silence grew, and I began to worry about my absence from my duties. Feeling it would be best if I were to say something, I said, "Might I have the honour of speaking to Mr Philip Gunn, sir?" He continued staring at the house, as though he were outside a criminal den of some sort.

"Most folk don't call it an honour, Jeeves." I was somewhat taken aback by this, and the silence grew once more. "You really think he's bought it?"

"Who, sir? Bought what?" Looking back, I am most embarrassed by my not recognising the slang for M. Hugo's death. However, you will remember that at the time I was quite flustered and feeling a little odd at the stillness of the man.

"The Frenchie."

"Monsieur Hugo, sir? I believe he was Belgian."

"Huh. No kidding." At this, Mr Gunn climbed out of his automobile. "He speak German?"

As an authority on M. Hugo's adventures, I felt a little more confident in answering the question, even if it did still strike me as bizarre. "I don't believe so sir."

"Yeah, you're looking at the reason why," said Mr Gunn, tossing his cigarette and striding towards the house. I confess I was shocked. Before I could think of a response, he had gone.

Mr Toomes arrived next, accompanied as always by Dr Johnson. The two bachelors had left their shared flat in central London and arrived in St Mary's by train.

"Mr Toomes!" I exclaimed, perhaps a little louder than I intended, but I was delighted to see in person the man who'd been on the front page so often. He gave me a cold look and flicked his walking stick aggressively towards the manor.

"Is this the Barnett Manor, my good man?"

"Indeed sir. Might I—" He started walking away before I could even finish speaking. Aside from a rather curt "Come, Johnson" directed to the doctor, who sheepishly followed him into the manor, the man didn't utter another word. As for M. Dupé, though a mere butler, I confess I was rather disappointed in meeting him. He seemed a somewhat dull, elderly man waiting to lecture anyone that would stand near him long enough.

Eventually, I informed the guests that the service would be commencing shortly. Immediately, Mr Gunn, Mr Toomes and M. Dupé visibly brightened, having previously been engaged in making snide remarks about the guests' sleeping habits and personal appearances.

The next events are rather painful to relate, but I feel it necessary to do so.

The three somehow managed to get to the front of the large crowd gathering at the church. The service was pleasant, with many eulogies and tributes to the great man, however I could not help but feel a creeping sense of apprehension looking at the detectives, who all seemed rather impatient. At the service's conclusion, a few guests mingled to pay their respects, and the detectives waited longer than any of them, with my lady and I remaining behind in our capacity as hosts. M. Hugo's coffin had been left in the church, as the little graveyard would have been swamped, and often it's a most emotional thing to witness a burial, so my lady and Captain Heathfield had thought it best to lay the legend to rest in a quieter, more discrete manner. There were the three detectives, Lady Barnett and the Captain standing by the coffin.

"Johnson," said Mr Toomes, "I have been patient enough."

"Well, I say Toomes, don't you think we ought to wait a little longer?" asked Dr Johnson, stammering somewhat as he did so.

"Nonsense! If anyone stands a chance of deducing who killed Hugo, it's me. Let's open the coffin." At this, there was naturally some considerable shock from my lady, the Captain and myself. However, M. Dupé's rather loud scoff was the most audible of reactions, and Mr Toomes turned to him and said, "Is there something that amuses you, sir?"

"Forgive me, my friend," replied the Frenchman quietly. "It is just so simple. I am surprised you have not already guessed who has done it. I only journeyed here to confirm my suspicions."

THE FUNERAL OF MONSIEUR HUGO

At this, Mr Gunn said to M. Dupé "Well, monsewer, my money's on a dame. Most of my cases, there's a dame at the root of the problem."

"Yes," said Mr Toomes, advancing on the coffin, "I wonder why."

"You got somethin' to say Toomes?"

Here my lady said: "Really, gentlemen!"

"Sorry if I shocked you Toots, but I never managed to stick my time at finishing school." The Captain turned red, and I confess I felt a strong urge to reprimand Mr Gunn. "Aha!" cried Mr Toomes. He had forced open the coffin, and was inspecting M. Hugo's head. "Dagger. Oriental design. Bejewelled handle." At this, M. Dupé snorted.

"Oriental design, Toomes? Are you so sure?"

Mr Toomes glared at M. Dupé, then returned his gaze to the body. Dr Johnson coughed apologetically, looked at the floor, and said "I say, old man, do you think there's maybe a better ti—"

"Shut up Johnson!" shouted Mr Toomes into the corpse of M. Hugo.

"Right ho," said Dr Johnson, perhaps a little hastily.

"Oriental design," Toomes repeated, glancing at M. Dupé, "but English-made."

"Bravo," said the Frenchman drily. Mr Gunn was now also peering in at the body.

"Definitely a dame. Back of the head, stab wound like that. One helluva angry broad. You can never trust em'."

"Please wait for your turn, sir," said Mr Toomes, elbowing Mr Gunn in the ribs. "This is all confirming my theory."

"Watch it, limey!" Mr Gunn snapped, grabbing Mr Toomes's midsection roughly, at which the Captain, who had been hovering, struggling with his thoughts, said "gentlemen, please! There is a lady present."

"This is a crime scene!" Mr Toomes snarled, grabbing the coffin to resist Mr Gunn.

"This is a funeral!" I cried, joining Mr Gunn's efforts.

After this, my memory is something of a blur. There was a lot of shouting and something hit me on the back of the head, and I awoke the next morning in my bedroom to learn of the fight that had broken out. Mr Toomes accused M. Dupé of the murder, M. Dupé revealed he had taken an item of M. Hugo's that apparently proved the Captain's guilt, and Mr Gunn produced a firearm and pointed it at Lady Barnett, accusing her of being involved.

Named, but as Mr Gunn, Mr Toomes and M. Dupé are currently pending bail for assault and stealing from a crime scene, I thought an account would prove useful for the police.

ARTEFACTS
Minty Taylor

<u>I</u>

i wonder who has you now
and what they might think to do with you,
and what they might think of your contents.
sorry. not contents. art. maybe.
but it is not yours, how can it be?

you are the tree upon which
the lovers carved their initials
but what do you matter when they
have fallen out of love? the sketches
on your skin will fade and your spine
will fray until the binding ceases,

leaving your pages to scatter
and decay.

<u>II</u>

and you. your silence haunts us.
i am so sorry you were
interrupted. you had become

such an orator when, not long before,
you could barely speak. no gentle
weeping now. better to stay silent.

III

i don't want to know what happened to you.
i only hope the drugs made you look
as old as you ought to have been when you
stopped.

i hope your black beard is white.
i hope your smooth skin now sags.

i hope you are as aged as your
stillness has made me. o body,

i beg you, turn to soil
beneath a yew tree.
at least then you might
give a long life to something.

CALLING OUT
Minty Taylor

You, page of possibility,
of intentionality and yet, also, accidents,
with your dishonest blankness
filled with bumps and creases
and grease from my fingers,
and the gravity that pulls my pen
away from a margin you didn't put
there but that I have been trained
to see by those who told me off
for colouring outside of the lines;

you, the undecaying remnant
of a living, breathing thing,
so crafted that I might taint
or adorn or tattoo with some
vain hope of meaning or speaking,
without sound but with implied noise
that might further imply, who
I talk to now and yet talk through
or past to talk to anyone else
who might not quite listen
but repeat; you, who is

so incapable of saying anything back
and yet instruct; you who is

thicker, more tangible than you
are given credit for, please
tell me what you want to hear.
 I will try to get it right this time.

KALEIDOSCOPE
Sandra Tse

The scars on his cracked heels move in and out of focus. A school of canary-yellow fish slide past. The ground rises beneath them. He is getting ahead.

Renee grabs at her dad's legs. His voice is mumbled against the ocean's roar, but she ignores it, climbing over him, the pulse of the waves hurling her onto the beach. She shivers, enjoying the thrill of winning.

Her dad lands with a thump next to her, wheezing. "Is that how you people… win… your competitions?"

"I don't know. We're usually the ones ahead."

He chuckles. White foam rushes towards them. Laughter and screams echo from beyond the rumble of the water, where other tourists are still swimming.

"Except at the interschool tournament," Renee adds. "We realised we didn't have enough banh khot for everyone at the tournament, and coach said I must have left some at home, but I swore I didn't. You saw me go out the door. Turns out Jeffrey ate five extra."

"Yeah? They must have been good."

Renee stands up, brushing herself off.

They haven't travelled for a long time. She remembers sitting on her dad's shoulders, surrounded by icy Scottish moors, and his hand holding hers as they leant against the railings of the Grand Canyon. She remembers when they used to make cup phones together and her dad sketched stingrays on them. They had known each other so well.

The seawater made her hair a tropical rainforest. She tucks a lock behind her ear, but jerks back immediately. Sunlight had painted a band of tanned skin around the place her ring belongs. Except the finger is unadorned. She rubs her hands, turns them over.

"Ray, you alright?"

Her dad lifts himself up on his elbows.

"I – you know, I never told you what tablecloth we ended up using."

"For the banh khot?" Her dad squints into the sun. "Ah, I get it now! Your team must have won all those competitions because you used the rulebook as tablecloth," he jokes.

Beyond him, golden rays reflect off the sand, sand that melts into the clear water like butter. This year her parents let her organise their entire Malaysian trip, since all mum wants to do is lay around at the hotel, getting spa treatments. They're supposed to be at the restaurant already, to escape the dinnertime crowd.

The shoreline is dull, natural, the sand almost undisturbed. Her stomach churns in a whirlpool. She sees herself on the Underground, reading her debate notes on her phone as the early morning rushes by.
A new wave pushes onto the shore, hissing as the water slides back into the depths again.

"Dad, I…" She swallows. "I can't find grandma's ring."

He sits up, brows pushed together under the weight of the sun.

"You sure? When was the last time you saw it?" he asks.

"Well, if I knew that then I would've known where it is now. Why would I ask? Can't you just help me find it?"

Swimmers crawl to shore, splashing about where the clear diamond surface deepens into blue-green. Renee digs her fingers into the sand, overturning pebbles and seashells. As the seawater dries off, the humidity patches her skin with stickiness. But after twenty minutes, her dad is following the other tourists back inland. Renee straightens. His lips are pressed into a thin line.

"Ray, it's such a tiny thing. It wasn't even that expensive."

"But grandma gave the ring to me." She rubs her hands together, her pulse beating in her fingertips. "When I was thirteen, remember?"

"We're never going to find it if it's in the water." He sighs. "Let's just enjoy the rest of the trip, eh?"

"Grandma's had it since she was a teenager. It's the only thing we have left from Saigon, since the war…"

"Don't worry about it, Ray. My father used to buy loads of chunky things for her, designer stuff. Listen, didn't you pick out a restaurant near here? I'm starving."

"It's… yes."

Her toes are cold. He had congratulated her when, after getting her first job, grandma gave her the ring to celebrate. And he had been there the night before she started eighth-grade at a new school. He brought her goi cuon rolls, protecting the plastic packaging from wet, stormy London in his jacket. He had laughed when she made up stories about who their ancestors might be, seeming to enjoy them, at the time.

The restaurant is a bamboo roof supported by a dozen pillars, chaperoned by plastic potted plants. Malaysian flags and flyers for various sailing tours plasters every available surface, with models smiling out of them posed as tourists.

They have changed out of their swimsuits, though Renee's hair still reeks of the sea. Platefuls of grilled baby squid lie in front of them, white tentacles sprouting into the air. Fairy lights are taped across the wooden ceiling, dimmed into dark beads by the sky. Even though it's nearly seven, the sun gives no indication of going away.

Renee pokes at a squid with the tip of her skewer. "Dad, do you think I should make more banh khot next year?"

The murmurs of conversation in the restaurant is slow, punctuated only by a splash of laughter now and again. He takes a bite of shrimp before answering, "Next year?"

"For the annual interschool tournament with Dulwich College and St Catherine's?"

"Oh, yeah, right. You just make sure you don't let anyone put anything in there, eh? Fair competition."

Renee lays her elbows on the table. "I just want everyone to get a taste instead of one person hoarding everything. I told you this an hour ago. It was Jeffrey."

"Ray, honest, you've had so many tournaments…"

"Grandma would have remembered," she says. "Aren't you curious I'm doing for the tournament this year?"

"What is this about, Ray?"

The fairy lights reflect off his irises in warped colours, shielding the brown he inherited from his mother. Renee leans back in her chair.

"We should have spent more time finding the ring."

"You shouldn't worry about my mother. She's not a good influence." The edge of his lip lifts. "She's always going on about family pride. Who her great-grandparents were and all that. She still thinks she's an aristocrat, and you don't need to encourage her. Her idea of the 'family' has nothing to do with me, or your aunt, or your grandpa."

Flames creep under the skin of her neck. "That's a lie."

"My mother is still dreaming of gold and admiration. All this Vietnamese food you're providing to the swimming team? Don't let it get to your head, alright?"

Waiters flow past their table, uninterested.

When Renee was younger, she had followed her grandma around the house. Sometimes dad invited her over, collapsing from exhaustion after Renee had been up all night. She would watch the grand old lady lay out her jewellery, sparkling jade and emeralds. She can still see grandma giving advice to her dad and aunt in a calm, dignified voice. Watched her nimble fingers, wrinkled with age, separating the rice paper for spring rolls.

"I want to make sure you're alright," he says.

It was her dad who had been furious with her when she was expelled. He convinced mum they should stop travelling and focus on Renee's 'education'. It hadn't been her fault. But he spent all summer after seventh-grade staring over her shoulder instead of looking in her eyes.

She studies his heavy-lidded eyes, and the crow's feet surrounding them. The couple at the next table are whispering loudly, staging a showcase of their perfect romance over the carcasses of shrimps and lobsters. After a while, her father starts talking about what souvenirs he wants to bring home to her aunt. Renee excuses herself to the toilet.

A small queue is forming outside the restaurant. The sun spotlights the people's faces, curious eyes peering at the seats. A kid's cheap balloon shark bobs in the air.

Soft clouds survey their own reflection on the ocean's surface as she follows the coastline, tracing back the way they came. Shops and restaurants line the edge of the shore, burning like a row of lightbulbs until they disappear around the bend of the bay.

They're going scuba diving tomorrow. She had booked their places months in advance. It was cheap. Her dad said he was looking forward to it. People move pass, as if in a kaleidoscope, blank faces masked by phones and cameras. Neon shopfronts and stalls appear then fall away.

The edge of the beach is inked brown by the water. A group of college kids lingered there, daring each other to go into the water. Every one of them clad in sequined dresses with ruby painted lips. One of them, balancing like a tightrope walker on her high heels, dips her toe in. The rest of her group screams.

"Ray."

Renee startles. She reaches for her ring as she turns, but feels only skin. Her dad stands a few steps away, with his hands in the pockets of his shorts, his duffle bag slung across one shoulder.

He nods at her, "You can't just run away like that."

Renee glances at the partygoers. She didn't expect him to come after her so quickly, and he wasn't making any jokes. She tucks her hair behind her ears. "I need the ring."

"Why?"

She glares at his t-shirt, rising and falling with his breath. "I don't expect you to understand."

It wasn't Renee's fault that the rest of the class agreed with her instead of that girl. The girl she had to work with in seventh-grade Physics was an idiot. Renee had to point out all her mistakes again, and again, and again. She was revolting, with acne scarring her face with red, as if all the stupidity was trying to crawl its way out from beneath her skin.

"I can't understand if you don't explain." His voice is stony, like thickened cement. "You're tired and upset. Let's get back to the hotel."

She bites the inside of her cheek. "You've never really understood, have you."

"If –"

"You still blame me for being expelled. You don't get it. You never really tried to understand. Ever. You-" She stops. Deep lines chisel his forehead. He can say it isn't true, but he said himself that he finds the ring pretentious.

"Ray – Re – listen to me," His voice is barely audible above the waves. The partygoers have moved further along the beach. She looks up.

"That was my fault," he says. "I raised you, of course I don't blame you for that. You're my daughter. Renee, I love you no matter what, alright?"

Renee tries to lift the corner of her lips. But her muscles won't move. The sky is dimming, the ocean a table of velvet. For months after the expulsion, she heard nothing from him but sighs and monosyllabic answers.

Her grandma didn't blame her at all. That idiot girl was only useful as comic relief, to relieve Renee from the pressure of the Physics project. Renee did everything. And what did the girl do instead of working? Cried and ran to mummy. She got Renee expelled. Pathetic.

I love you no matter what. Her dad's words drag at her chest, as she walks towards the sea. The icy water seeps into her sneakers, sloshing against the ankles of her jeans.

All the ideas she had of impressing her school lie rotting amongst the broken shells and pebbles. She stares down at his blurred outline on the waves. She wants to remember what it's like to whisper into a cup phone, just the two of them in a tent fort in the middle of the living room. But it felt as distant now as the horizon. Over the expanse of grey, the sun dresses the world in a glitter of crimson and gold, a tent pulled over the sky.

MODERN MELANCHOLY
Jess Watts

On our knees,
Begging for validation, not water–
The trivialised murdering of ourselves,
Lines that the crowd draws, off across structures
("that's it, your aspiration")
Relief aid in an alphabet – f for failure,
Try better: emotions in emoticons
But Sadness: the product of x
The traversed poverty line–
Student debt, real debt, life-savings, we're insatiable;
Lock the piggy bank, we're cautious.

Poured onto forgotten blogs,
Our inexpressive thoughts are read, in the dark,
And love, the human kind–
A disregard– the slippery disconnect of our showered
Limbs, drinking to numb, not sustain
And we see more of that world with every season change;
Addictions,
And the simple nature
That seeks to write us all in song.

Institutions; uniforms worn like inmates,
Competitive salary, mortgage, pension– fine cloth– gold dust to those
Under the sun, in mud, privilege like sand;
Scrolling to replace memory as we tell the world our woes,
Ask voids, the pretend audience,
Those ticker taped-lives, re-living,
But nothing stays a moment: not anymore,
Survival conquered; and next?

Inject,
Swallow, the shedding of skin,

Charity of social invitation, eye contact– fleeting– of course– hesitation
To be human, and disasters
That rip minds, our homes intact,
We're the prisoners of a war:
Fulfilment and expectation found silently,
Folded patiently,
Into corners.

HOLY MARY, MOTHER MARY
Nyree Williams

'Hail Mary,
Full of Grace,
The Lord is with thee,
Blessed art thou amongst women,
And Blessed is the fruit of thy womb,
Jesus,
Holy Mary,
Mother of God,
Pray for us sinners now and at the hour of our death,
Amen.'

*

Mother Mary sits in her celestial armchair listening to the last of her world's children say their prayers. She is dressed in a grey pinafore and labor-stained apron. Her face is lined with the weight of the world, whilst her eyes, full of something inexpressible, look far off into the distance. A quilt flows down from her soft lap. It is alive with scenes of toil and grit, of domesticity and comfort, of motherhood. She closes her eyes, runs her calloused, wise hands over the quilt, and sticks in the needle.

*

No. 2 The Oval,
Warley
Birmingham

Inside a terraced two-up two-down with a fence at the front and a long, thin stretch of lawn at the back, my grandmother, Winnie, puts her six-year-old twins to bed. After fussing over the blackout curtains, Winnie makes to leave, but is stopped by a call from my father.

When will the rabbits on the wall be papered over? Can it be tomorrow?

The rabbits scare him. They grow to inexpressible sizes and chase him in strange, psychedelic nightmares. His brother giggles beside him and Winnie expresses a similar amount of sympathy. My father sulks, and with a distrustful look at the garish rabbits papered just above the dado rail... directly above his head, assents to a kiss from his mother, who again goes over to re-adjust the curtains for it is always the last thing she does. After having drawn them at least a centimetre closer, she turns the light off and heads downstairs.

On her way, she passes the wood-framed oil painting of Jesus her husband bought for her at the rag market. His crimson cloak is made of velvet, and the colour of his hair mixes in with the gold ring of light emanating from his halo-topped head. His one hand is outstretched towards her, beckoning, whilst the other lays across the sacred heart. He sits crookedly, an unsettling reminder of the bombing only a few days ago which took down the water tower across the road. She sighs and straightens the painting before touching the cross around her neck and uttering a small prayer. She is thankful that her husband's bad lungs kept him from the war, and she is thankful that the fire he helped put out didn't kill him either. She is snapped out of her reverie by a knock at the door.

A man in a wool suit stands on the doorstep. Clipboard in hand. Winnie thinks she recognises him as Someone Important but can't be sure. She straightens first her spine, then her skirt, and locks her eyes onto his. He is well-spoken, and her Birmingham accent sounds crude to her own ears in comparison. She should have scrubbed the doorstep this morning. Pointing to a name-tag pinned to his lapel, he introduces himself as Mr. Tanner, he is her local MP, and he has come in regard to the recommended evacuation of school-age children from the UK's major cities into the countryside...

And Winnie stops listening.

*

It is early September 1936, Winnie sits in her living room rubbing goose fat onto her sons' tiny chests. When the swaddled bundles are coated, she places them side by side under another blanket in the dresser drawer in front of the fire. One is bluish and one is yellow. They are twins and premature. They are not expected to survive very long.

On her mind is the task at hand. Next, she must find names, and quickly. The boys need christening, quickly.

She feels her husband's hand come to rest on her shoulder. Her body tenses under the weight of his care, and the rejection comes out of her involuntarily. She brushes him off and walks into the kitchen. She must find names. And she must do tea. Her husband, with eyes shining, looks from his sickly sons to his narrow-framed wife rooting in the cupboards. Winnie turns around and walks briskly back into the living room with a tin of corned beef. "Douglas and Donald," she reads triumphantly from the label.

"That's what we'll call them."

Her husband stands gawping at his wife and wonders at what victory she feels she's won.

Winnie looks questioningly back at him; at least they'll get to heaven.

*

Mr. Tanner looks pleased with himself, Winnie's absence has allowed him to gesticulate wildly at his new-found ally on The Dangers of War. When he informs her that the children will be evacuated from the school in a week's time, Winnie politely declines what doesn't seem a choice. Mr. Tanner stands aghast, and there is a small silence before he regains his composure. Need he remind her, that they are living in a warzone? My grandmother, with her eyes on a mark on the doorstep replies that yes, she is quite aware.

And may he ask, for what reason she refuses to send her children to safety? And may he just take the time to explain that the water tower won't be the only thing to go? And was she aware that the government had everybody's best interests at heart?

Winnie is stunned into submission. More than anyone, she knows how bad it's got, her husband risked his life putting out the fire when the water tower went up. But what kind of mother would she be if she sent her children away to strangers? They could be anyone. This is their home, where they're meant to be.

Mr. Tanner continues with his tirade, and, could he counter, how guilty would she feel, if her children died because she couldn't face sending them away? Did she not think, perhaps, that she was being a little selfish?

Something stirs in the pit of my grandmother's stomach, and her eyes bore into the doorstep stain. The painting of Jesus begins to form in it, only in his hand is a pot of goose fat. He slathers her in it and pulls her in. He watches over her whilst she joins a thousand freakishly large rabbits with signs chanting along a picket line. One of them wordlessly presses a corned beef tin into her hands and it slices her.

My grandmother raises her eyes to meet Mr. Tanner's, and replies: "We might bloody well die. But if we do, at least we'll all die together. Right here, underneath the kitchen table."

And with that, Mr. Tanner finally leaves, mumbling indiscreetly as he does so, and Winnie heads back into her home, closing the door firmly behind her.

*

Mother Mary ties the final knot and allows herself a weary smile. All across the world, mothers good and mothers bad are making choices for better, and for worse.

And Mother Mary witnesses it all, and her immortal stitches engrain them into the fabric of the world so that they are remembered forever.

HUMAN
Alex Wiseman

SOLAR
    Do you hate yourself?
LUNAR
    I'm sorry?
SOLAR
    Don't you know what that means?
LUNAR
    Yes, of course. Of course I know what it means. Just, why?
SOLAR
    Why what?
LUNAR
    Why are you asking me that?
SOLAR
    Because I want to know.
LUNAR
    Know what?
SOLAR
    If you hate yourself. Or not.
LUNAR
    Why do you want to know that?
SOLAR
    Because I think I know the answer, and I want to check.
LUNAR
    Well, uh, I don't know. I haven't thought about it much, I suppose. I don't love myself, sure, but hate?
SOLAR
    Well what do you hate?
LUNAR
    Swimming. My brother. Being stuck in a queue when I'm late for something. Most fruit. Ad breaks on TV. My lack of empathy. My abundance of dependencies. Losing one of my favourite sock. Involuntary social gatherings. Summer. The idea of heaven. The colour purple.

SOLAR
>	Purple?

LUNAR
>	Yeah.

SOLAR
>	But that's a strong, regal colour.

LUNAR
>	Yeah.

SOLAR
>	Right. Well. Think about how you feel about those things. How much you hate them. Really let it sink in. Now think about yourself. Does how you view yourself, how you feel about yourself resemble, at all, how you feel about those other things?

LUNAR
>	I suppose so.

SOLAR
>	There you go. I was right. You hate yourself.

Some time. SOLAR *nudges* LUNAR.

LUNAR
>	What?

SOLAR
>	Ask me.

LUNAR
>	Ask you what?

SOLAR
>	The question.

LUNAR
>	What question?

SOLAR
>	The one I asked you.

LUNAR
>	Why?

SOLAR
>	It's only polite.

LUNAR
>	Okay. Sure. Do you hate yourself?

SOLAR
>	God no! No, I love myself, utterly. I mean I have imperfections, sure, but I love those too. It's like I'm some sort of carnival big–

top, spewing out bright lights and self-esteem. And I've got all the different acts inside me. The lions and the dancers and the clowns, all muddled and mixed up into one. I think you need to love yourself, because love is longevity with fewer letters. It su stains you. Keeps you going. To someone with a hammer, everything starts to look like nails. To someone with hate in their heart, everything starts to look like a way out. But to someone with love in the place of hate, everything starts to look bright and beautiful and worthwhile. *(Pause)* I got carried away, sorry.

LUNAR
    It's okay.

Some time.

SOLAR
    Do you like your body?
LUNAR
    What?
SOLAR
    Your body.
LUNAR
    Yes?
SOLAR
    Do you like it?
LUNAR
    Like? What do you mean by like?
SOLAR
    Are you content with your body? Is it adequate? Or do you hate it, too? Can you pick things out, point at them, pinch them, poke them, that you wish were not the way they are?
LUNAR
    Different?
SOLAR
    What?
LUNAR
    Do I wish my body was different?
SOLAR
    Yes.
LUNAR
    Or am I content with it?

SOLAR
>Yes.

Some time. LUNAR *thinks.*

LUNAR
> I wish I were a bird.

SOLAR
> A bird?

LUNAR
> Yes.

SOLAR
> What kind?

LUNAR
> Any kind. A small one.

SOLAR
> Why?

LUNAR
> Because they can sing. All birds sing. No matter where or how or by what cosmic circumstances brought them into existence. They sing, and it is beautiful. They sing, and all the other birds understand. They sing, and even if their song is stripped away from their feathers and fragile bones, they still could, at some point, no matter what, sing. I don't have anything like that. If you take me away from this body, this personality, this consciousness, there is nothing. I am nothing, there is no song. I am no bird. I am a body with a voice and nothing more. If I were a bird it'd be simple. The bird is scared of the cat,
> the cat is scared of the dog, the dog is scared of the
> man, the man is scared of– what?– himself?
> God? The apocalypse? Forgetting a birthday? Their own body? I am.

SOLAR
> What?

LUNAR
> I'm scared.

SOLAR
> Of what?

LUNAR
> My body.

SOLAR
> In what way?

LUNAR
> I've got wishbones in my arms, and dandelion stalks in my legs. I've got stubbornness in my blood, ill-worded and poorly-thought-out judgements in my spit, and hope where I don't dare look. There's a forest—

SOLAR
> A forest?

LUNAR
> A dark forest in my belly. Maybe a jungle. Self-absorption, hatred and tigers thrive there. I'm growing quite tired of all the roaring.

SOLAR
> So you hate your body as well as yourself?

LUNAR
> What?

SOLAR
> You hate your body?

LUNAR
> I suppose so. I look in a mirror and I see eyes loaded with thunder, skin that tells the story of a thousand yesterdays, and not a bird in sight.

SOLAR
> That's a shame.

Some time. SOLAR *nudges* LUNAR.

LUNAR
> What about you?

SOLAR
> I love my body. I adore it. I cherish it and care for it and protect it. My body isn't a temple, it's a religion. It's got doctrines to follow, ideals, martyrs, and the power to control and contort so many things. My fingers make steeples under which people are married and buried. My eyes are the pools of holy water where innocence is baptised. My feet are the communities that make the most of their faith, and make it more than it ever could be as faith alone. The future is beautiful, and I, my body, is it.

LUNAR
> It?

SOLAR
> The future. My body is the future of myself and it is beautiful. It is a prolepsis into what will be; it's the bud of a rose, the feather of a peacock, grapes on a vine. We are celestial creatures. People looked

up into the night sky and saw themselves in the constellations. We are stars. We burn and burn and burn, so beautifully, until we explode in a supernova, in death, our spectacular death. But we burn so bright, with so much inspiration and fantasy that people will remember us. Whatever happens, people will remember us and our bodies. In an urn, under a slab of stone. We are memorable creatures with bodies made for expression. *(Pause)* I got carried away, sorry.

LUNAR

No, it's okay. It's just-

SOLAR

Just what? Do you not agree?

LUNAR

I'm surprised is all.

SOLAR

Surprised?

LUNAR

I'm surprised when someone tells me that they're happy.

SOLAR

I never said I was happy.

LUNAR

Well when they say they like their own bodies. I'm surprised. Happiness is a rarity. True happiness. Happiness of the soul, not of the moment. It seems to have become something fleeting and flimsy, like a new relationship or that jump in your stomach with small excitements. I'm not surprised by depression anymore. Not because I think it's cool, because I don't, because it isn't. It's not a fad, it's not fashionable or romantic or something to try and attain, maintain, or become akin to. It's brutal, and boring, and bloody heart-breaking. It's being chewed to death by your own toothless and blind dog. But with a body like mine–

SOLAR

A body like yours?

LUNAR

Yes.

SOLAR

Like what?

LUNAR

A body.

SOLAR

What is your body like?

LUNAR

Alive. Normal. Extraordinary. Human.

SOLAR

    Right.

LUNAR

    With a body like this, one that I half-heartedly hate with all my heart, one that is so well equipped for self-destruction there might as well be a big red button on the back of my neck, one that is comfortable in the chains of self-consciousness, one that is not itself an anti depressant for itself or any other body, one that both breeds and butchers empathy, one that is a pyre with fuel of expectations and flame of blood-red disappointments, one that lives through obligations to itself, one that is but a speck of dust in this exodus of self-satisfaction, with a body such as this it is difficult to want to live in it.

SOLAR

    I don't think so.

LUNAR

    You don't?

SOLAR

    No, not at all.

LUNAR

    How so?

SOLAR

    We are not our bodies. We are not our consciousnesses. We are not ourselves. We are, at best, human. And that is an incomprehensibly incredible thing.

LUNAR

    Human, at best?

SOLAR

    Is there anything better? For us, as humans, is there anything better, anything higher for us to aspire to be than what we already are?

LUNAR

    A bird?

SOLAR

    This is bigger than birds. This is bigger than fish or mammals or microbes. We are human, and we don't give ourselves enough credit for that. In this universe of infinity and specificity, we exist and are alive and are the most complicated, intelligent beings we know of. Somehow, out of stardust or bone or sheer determination we exist in these our bodies with blood as red as the suns heart in our veins, and an imagination filled with gardens and toads and memories of sleepovers and the names of childhood toys.

LUNAR
> None of that equals happiness.

SOLAR
> What?

LUNAR
> None of that means that we have to be happy. There's nothing ingrained within us for that to be a permanence or an obligation. All of that may be so, but it doesn't mean that we're happy. I'm not.

SOLAR
> I don't understand.

LUNAR
> How so?

SOLAR
> Why concern yourself with happiness? What is it? Why does it matter when we are beings that deserve nought but awe?

LUNAR
> Because we're, at best, human. And, with humanity, comes a desire to be happy. We cannot live off of awe alone. We have a furnace in our chests that spits out all fuels bar happiness, bar small smiles, bar thoughtfulness, bar sympathy, bar hugs and friends and dogs and birthdays and confidence and contentment. Water, Oxygen, Food, Happiness. It's a necessity, I think. And it all boils down to the body. Because I think that we are our bodies. We're all-too-familiar with the chinks of steel and the mottled boughs of ourselves, that if we don't like that, how are we going to be happy? It is our immediate, unchangeable environment that dictates how we live in more ways than are fair by any standards. We must concern ourselves with becoming happy, with liking the vessels in which we reside, with dealing with the world in which we inhabit, with comprehending this our universe of man-made constellations and impossibility. Because if we don't, then we simply aren't human, and then we're nothing but dust that wants to sing.

Some time.

SOLAR
> *(tenderly)* Do you hurt yourself?

LUNAR
> What?

SOLAR
> Do you burn, cut or bruise yourself? You said you had a body well-equipped for self-destruction, but do you?

LUNAR
> Do I what?

SOLAR
> Self-destruct, ever?

LUNAR
> Why do you ask?

SOLAR
> Because I think I know the answer, and I want to check.

Some time.

LUNAR
(nodding gently) Yes. I do.

SOLAR *goes to* LUNAR *and hugs them.* LUNAR *sobs. Linger on this.*

LUNAR
> I just–

SOLAR
> It's okay.

LUNAR
> I get so angry–

SOLAR
> It's alright.

LUNAR
> And I don't know how to–

SOLAR
> You don't have to say anything. You don't need to have anything powerful or of impact to say. You don't have to have poetry for this.

Curtain.

AUTHOR BIOGRAPHIES

Beth Bacon
Beth is a third year English Literature student. She was born in East London but brought up in Lancashire. Beth began writing poetry at the age of 14. She moved onto playscripts when she was 16 and has focussed on prose since being at UEA. 'It's Not Going To End This Way' was inspired by a passionate interest in True Crime, theatre, and The Talented Mr Ripley.

Geronimo Bennington-Poulter
Geronimo is the eldest of eight children but not the tallest or brightest. Traditionally, the eldest in his family becomes a cobbler (the second eldest a baker, the third a farrier and the fourth an idiot). Geronimo has broken from tradition and decided to pursue a career in writing. His writing style is deeply inspired by the allergy warnings on the back of Bachelor's soup boxes.

Meghalee Bose
Maghalee is a fourth-year undergraduate student, completing a semester of exchange at UEA. She lives in Melbourne and is majoring in Creative Writing and Computer Science at La Trobe University. Speculative fiction mashed with realism is her area of interest. She sometimes moonlights as a playwright, and has won the Geoffrey Milne Student Theatre grant from her university for scriptwriting, with her work also having been included in past productions of La Trobe Student Theatre.

Ciara Bright
Ciara is in her second year of the Creative Writing course, and splits her time between dancing and writing. Ciara writes a lot of poetry to read at open mic nights, and has published selections of poems both online and in anthologies. Her favourite thing to write is fantasy prose, taking inspirations from the likes of JRR Tolkien, CS Lewis, JK Rowling, and Diana Wynne Jones, as well as traditional fairy tales and mythology.

Sebastian Bronson-Boddie
Sebastian is a second-year Creative Writing student from the east coast of the United States. At home, they attend Goucher College, a small liberal arts institution in the suburbs of Baltimore. While their writing processes is erratic, their work is consistent in its overwhelming attention to image, concern with musicality, and nostalgia for the small dramas of everyday life.

Hannah Brown
Raised along the windy south coast, Hannah likes to write about history and murder, so romance is a little deviation from the norm; despite that, 'Change Here' is a favourite of the stories she's written. She is in her final year of the BA English Literature with Creative Writing degree, and hopes to continue reading and writing long after she graduates.

Lizzie Brown
Lizzie is a final year Drama student from West Yorkshire, and wrote 'Credible Fear' as a response to her part as Rose of Sharon in UEA Drama's production of The Grapes of Wrath. Normally more comfortable on the acting side of things, writing Credible Fear was a new venture for Lizzie – both in to play writing and in to the world of the emotional, dramatic, and up to date subject matter.

Amelia Court
Amelia, a third year English Literature student, loves a lot of things. These include oranges, the colour of wet grass under blue sky, McDonald's delivery service, when words sound good together, cold cider, crying at videos of dogs being reunited with their family, crying with laughter, crying, that feeling you get when one of your favourite songs turns up unexpectedly in a film, writing sad poetry, and a cardboard cut-out of Jake the Dog.

Grace Curtis
Grace is a geordie ex-pat currently completing her third year at UEA. Her interests include magical realism, space cowboys, and rock climbing. She is also the author of a webcomic called *SUPERFREAKZ* which she will take any opportunity to shamelessly promote.

Alice Davies
Alice is from Maidenhead and is a second-year English Literature with Creative Writing student. She mostly writes poetry and short stories, inspired by the world around her but also the inner mind. Alice enjoys travelling because it changes her mindset and allows her to focus on a new perspective when writing. Music is really important to her as both an escape and lyrical inspiration (and she loves metaphors a bit too much).

Dylan Davies
Dylan, a first year English Literature and Creative Writing student, made a promise at the age of nine or ten that they would only ever read Jacqueline Wilson novels and write stories about vampires. Something clearly went askew somewhere, because now, for better or for worse, they write poetry.

Ella Dorman-Gajic
Ella is a poet, playwright and actor studying Scriptwriting and Performance. Her debut spoken word show 'Did I Choose These Shoes?' was on at Brighton & Edinburgh Fringe. She has performed her poetry around the country, including at Wise Words, That's What She Said and UniSlam. Currently, she is Writer in Residence for Broken Silence Theatre, who produced her play 'Trust', on at London's Old Red Lion Theatre; she working with them on developing her new play 'Divided'.

Frankie Finch
Frankie, who frequently goes by Sharkfinstew on social media, is an incredibly dark poet, focusing mostly on the macabre and mythological. For her, poetry is an expression of the darkest parts of people and an exploration of different philosophical ideas. Her work is heavily inspired by postmodern writers such as Simon Armitage and Vicki Feaver.

Jessica Firman
Jessica is a second year English Literature with Creative Writing student. Originating from Essex, she started writing in order to improve her creative writing portion of the English Language GSCE. She used to run a weekly writing blog, but now - having shifted her focus more to poetry - she runs a poetry account on Instagram, though still writes prose. Usually writing more serious pieces, this was her debut for comedic writing.

Willa Froy
Willa does not know what to write in her biography. After asking everyone she still has not found a conclusion, except that she really loves the sea which she hopes will wash away her bio worries.

Sam Gardham
Sam Gardham is a first-year on the English and Creative Writing BA. He is 20 and comes from Watford, which has the rare honour of being, to his knowledge, the only town apart from Doncaster that's been dissed in the poetry of Simon Armitage. Sam writes stories, sometimes with the intention of making himself laugh. They tend to be slightly peculiar in one way or another.

Kasper Hassett
Kasper is a first year student of English literature with creative writing at UEA, originally from London. He usually writes prose and 'Theatre' is one of his first attempts at poetry. One of his greatest fixations in writing is the unconventional presentation of atmosphere, and how perspective can alter this.

Maya Hayes
Maya is an English Literature and Creative Writing student in her third year. Her writing tends to reflect an interest in realism, minimalism and gender dynamics.

Judith Howe
Judith is a third year English Literature student at UEA. Her writing has appeared online through Young Poets Network as well as in print in *Underline: The UEA Undergraduate Anthology 2018* and *Volta: An Obscurity of Poets* published by SalóPress. She once wrote a comment piece for Concrete arguing that Christmas adverts are actually an art form, which really tells you all you need to know about her.

David Hubbard
David is a second year English Literature with Creative Writing student. In his writing he values intimacy with the kind of grounded characters you feel like you already know. His passion comes from unearthing the quiet little stories that subtly shape the world around us. While he loves writing short stories, he also spends much of his time writing children's fiction, scripts and novels.

Joe Hull
Joseph is a second-year creative writing student at UEA. Although inclusion in this publication represents his most prestigious life achievement to date, he maintains a youthful vigour and ready wit that more than compensate for his complete lack of future prospects. His writing has been variously described as "claustrophobic", "shamelessly derivative" and "almost unbearably depressing". In his spare time he enjoys binge drinking, gratuitous sarcasm and fruit yogurts.

Honor Leveson-Gower
Honor has lived her whole life on the Hebridean Island of North Uist off the West coast of Scotland. She takes inspiration from the surroundings she is so familiar with: The crystal white sand shoreline pounded by azure Atlantic waves. The Celtic Culture that envelopes the Islands people and traditions and the fantastic wildlife on the Land in the air and in the sea.

Dana Liew Qi-E
Dana is a permanently exhausted first year international English Literature and Creative Writing student. She enjoys writing prose fiction, and is currently making forays into interactive fiction and all the messiness that entails. Currently, the topics that she is taking a stab at including in her work are 'the role of choice in interactive media', 'representation' and 'umbrella cockatoos'.

Charles Lobo-Clarke
Charles is a second year English Literature & Creative Writing student. He enjoys writing both prose and poetry, he is also an upcoming Norwich stand-up comedian. His work tends to be characterized by themes of postcolonialism, environmental issues and inequality done in a humorous, bizarre, and surreal style.

Chris Matthews
Chris is a second year Literature and Creative Writing student from Reading. He has won awards including Category 2 of Beaumont Park's Poetry Trail (Huddersfield Literature Festival) for his poem 'Permanence', and the Young Poets Network's August Challenge #2 for 'Stairs'. He mainly writes natural lyrical verse, and the poet who inspires him most is Michael Longley. In his spare time he enjoys sailing and listening to the football.

Lucy May
It was in her final year of primary school that Lucy realised she'd like to be a writer. Ten years later, she still hasn't found anything else she'd rather do. When she isn't being President of UEA's Creative Writing Society, hosting workshops or helping craft anthologies, you can find her roaming the Derbyshire dales hunting down her next idea.

Magdalena Meza Mitcher
Magdalena is a born and raised Londoner, undergoing her second year on her English Literature with Creative Writing course. She is currently spending her time on a semester abroad in Spain, passing most days by drinking sangria and pretending to gain life experience to feed into her writing. She also runs a blog in her spare time (of which she has an abundance) where she posts sad poetry and the occasional short story.

Millie Norman
Millie is a first year English Literature with Creative Writing student from Woking. She mainly writes short experimental prose and performance poetry surrounding mental health, identity and relationships. She is also the blog editor and creative writing correspondent for international art collective *!GWAK*.

Amber Otton-Miller
Amber is a third year student of English Literature and Creative Writing. Her poetry is influenced by confessional and abstract styles, such as the work of Maggie Nelson, in which she hopes to convey a series of attitudes and emotions to one particular experience. She is currently working on a poetry and lyric essay collective focusing on the politics of the female body.

Cara Ow
Cara is a final year English Lit with Creative Writing student. She's a poet masquerading as a prose writer in this anthology… but should probably drop the act. Her work has appeared in last year's undergrad anthology *Underline,* UEA's *Diaspora Diaries* magazine and the Singaporean anthology *My Lot Is A Sky*. Cara also does events and graphic design on the Womanist Society committee, and compulsively sleeps in most (if any) of her spare time.

Amy Pattison
Amy is a third-year English literature student from Havering. She usually writes prose but has started writing poetry in the past year. This piece was written for a summative assessment last semester.

Flo Pearce-Higginson
Flo is in her first year, studying English Literature with Creative Writing. Originally from Devon, she enjoys writing naturalistic and surrealist writing, and hopes to one day be a successful author. She has adored books and writing her own stories from a very young age, and is very happy to be pursuing her dream at university.

Chiara Picchi
Chiara is a Second Year Literature and History student originally from Italy but raised in Luxembourg. She writes primarily prose and particularly short stories and flash fiction. She prefers to do so in English although French and Italian make an occasional appearance in her work. She enjoys exploring a wide variety of themes ranging from the supernatural to mental health.

John Raspin
John is a third year English Literature with Creative Writing student. He is deeply interested in all things old and believes that the past is an unfamiliar, alienating site which makes it the perfect setting for terrifying tales. With this in mind, his writing is defined by dark and gothic undertones and its building sense of dread. All in all, it's good bedtime reading!

Beth Reeves
Beth is a third year English Literature student, who enjoys writing poetry and short stories. Having grown up by the Cornish coast, she draws inspiration for her writing from the landscape and rural lifestyle. After studying a crime and detective fiction module in her final year, she has found a new interest in the genre and hopes to explore this more in her writing.

Ellie Reeves
Ellie is an up-and-coming poet and prose writer in her final year of English Literature and Creative Writing at the University of East Anglia. Her work harnesses magical realism to delve into themes surrounding the body, queerness and meta-poetry. Also an editor for Egg Box Publishing, Reeves is currently heading her first publication, Polari, in collaboration with young queer writers, and completing her debut dystopian novel.

George Rennison
George is a writer based in Norwich. He has written plays for UEA Drama Society and the New Wolsey Theatre, Ipswich and is the resident Musical Director of the award-winning Eastern Edge Theatre Company, who are premiering his new musical 'Berlin Girl' at this year's Edinburgh Fringe Festival. He appreciates a good cup of tea and apparently plays the piano too loudly for his neighbours.

Saskia Reynolds
Saskia is a first-year English Literature and Creative Writing student from London. Her writing tends to focus on people, their relationships and how they perceive the world around them. At the moment, her main inspiration comes from the works of Haruki Murakami, due to his ability to invoke empathy using straightforward yet deeply emotive language. She has a weakness for French idioms and characters who believe themselves to be ordinary.

Colin Sheehan
Colin is a third year English Literature with Creative Writing student. In his spare time he plays and runs Dungeons and Dragons campaigns. He normally writes satirical, speculative and horror-based stories. He is very good friends with a cat that lives at the edge of the Avenues, and can often be found chilling with her. This is his first time being published.

Minty Taylor
Minty's life is a mess. He can't remember the last time he said no to anything and hasn't washed his clothes in weeks. Minty writes poetry, prose and music and has performed around the country.
Last summer Minty toured the UK with a group of poets promoting the album Words w/ Friends Vol 3. This is his third appearance in the undergraduate anthology. He dedicates these poems to the memory of his friend Ted.

Sandra Tse
Sandra is a third-year student studying English Literature. A second-hand Dr. Seuss book sparked her interest in publishing when her mother mended a

missing page with pencil drawings and sellotape. She discovered her love for extended metaphors at UEA and continues to write prose that engages with myths and older texts. When not found with an iced coffee in the library, she is travelling around the UK.

Jess Watts
Jess is a second year English Literature with Creative Writing Student and long-time aspiring author – since she was six years old! When not in Norwich, she lives in South London and, after remembering that she's writing one, works on her novel. Jess enjoys characterisation and creating interactions between her characters. Occasionally she ventures into poetry and likes to write conceptual pieces that explore the contemporary world.

Nyree Williams
Nyree is a third year English Literature and Drama student from Wales. 'Holy Mary, Mother Mary' was inspired by stories she was told about her Grandmother's experience of the Second World War, and a fascination she began to have with motherhood and the differences in the expression and suppression of emotion now, and in the past. It is her first venture into prose writing, having previously only written short scripts and monologues.

Alexander Wiseman
Alexander is a second year Scriptwriting & Performance student from Chichester, West Sussex. He writes both poetry and script and is especially interested in merging the two forms – experimenting with structural and linguistic conventions. His short play 'Necronomicomedy' was recently performed in the UEA Drama Studio as part of the Drama Society's Spotlights Festival 2019. He was also part of the team representing UEA at the UniSlam 2019 spoken word competition in Birmingham.

This anthology also features the work of **Milo Filtness**, who did not provide an author bio.

ACKNOWLEDGEMENTS

Editor-in-Chief: Eve Mathews

Head of Design and Production: Francesca Giuliani

Head of Sales: Ellie Reeves

Head of Marketing: Alex Paulley

DESIGN AND PRODUCTION TEAM

Charlotte Brown
Jasmine Langcaster-James
Mireia Molina Costa

EDITORIAL TEAM

Aaron Blakesley
Abigail Braim
Alec Goldstone
Alice Kouzmenko
Amelia Court
Amelia Cox
Amy Pattison
Amy Ray
Ananya Wilson-Bhattacharya
Anastasia Christodoulou
Anisha Jackson
Beth Reeves
Caroline Moratti
Charlotte Brown
Colin Sheehan
Conor Smith
Daisy Flynn
Electra Nanou
Elif Soyler
Ella Rowdon
Ellie Reeves
Ellie Robson
Emily Gaskell
Emily Tsuchiya
Emma Bullen
Francesca Giuliani
Hannah Lee
James Hose
Jenna Gook
Joel Shelley
Johanne Elster Hanson
Josephine Nyeko-Lacek
Kate Robinson
Kitty Nash
Leon Lee
Lucy May
Lucy Peake
Max Pleasance
Mireia Molina Costa
Natalie Hemming
Oihane Garcia
Raphaelle Broughton
Rebecca Allen
Rebecca Blasdale-Smith
Rebecca Philips
Reeve Langston
Rowan Bryer
Ruby Pinner
Ruth Delany
Ryan Norman
Sasha Louise Durance
Sophie Rose-Land
Tony Allen

Undertone
First published by Egg Box Publishing 2019
Part of UEA Publishing Project Ltd
International ©2019 retained by individual authors
A CIP record for this book is available from the British Library

This book is sold subject to the condition that it shall not, by way of trade or otherwise, be lent, resold, hired out, stored in a retrieval system, or otherwise circulated without the publisher's prior consent in any form of binding or cover other than that in which it is published and without a similar condition including this condition being imposed on the subsequent purchaser.

Undertone is typeset in Garamond
Cover Design by Mireia Molina Costa ©2019
Typeset by Francesca Giuliani, with the assistance of Mireia Molina Costa, Jasmine Langcaster-James and Charlotte Brown
Printed and bound in the UK by Imprint Digital
Distributed by NBN International

ISBN 978-1911343677